Practical Sacramental Theology

Practical Sacramental Theology

At the Intersection
of Liturgy and Ethics

BRUCE T. MORRILL

 CASCADE *Books* · Eugene, Oregon

PRACTICAL SACRAMENTAL THEOLOGY
At the Intersection of Liturgy and Ethics

Cascade Books
An Imprint of Wipf and Stock Publishers
199 W. 8th Ave., Suite 3
Eugene, OR 97401

www.wipfandstock.com

PAPERBACK ISBN: 978-1-7252-9718-0
HARDCOVER ISBN: 978-1-7252-9719-7
EBOOK ISBN: 978-1-7252-9720-3

Cataloguing-in-Publication data:

Names: Morrill, Bruce T., author.

Title: Practical sacramental theology : at the intersection of liturgy and ethics / Bruce T. Morrill.

Description: Eugene, OR : Cascade Books, 2021 | Includes bibliographical references and index(es).

Identifiers: ISBN978-1-7252-9718-0 (paperback) | ISBN 978-1-7252-9719-7 (hardcover) | ISBN 978-1-7252-9720-3 (ebook)

Subjects: LCSH: Public worship. | Liturgics. | Christian Life. | Christian Theology. | Ethics.

Classification: BV178 .M69 2021 (paperback) | BV178 .M69 (ebook)

08/31/21

Contents

Acknowledgments

THE EIGHT CHAPTERS COMPRISING this book reproduce, with certain modifications of content and style, texts originally published in peer-reviewed journals and collective volumes. I am grateful to Peeters Publishers and Orbis Books for giving explicit permission to reuse my writings from their volumes. I am likewise thankful for the opportunities afforded me by the editors and publishers of *Studia Liturgica, Theological Studies, CTSA Proceedings*, and *NAAL Proceedings* for granting sole, post-publication rights to the content of my essays in their respective venues. The sources for each chapter are as follows:

Chapter 1: "Sacramental-Liturgical Theology Since Vatican II: The Dialectic of Meaning and Performance." *Proceedings of the Catholic Theological Society of America* 67 (2012) 1–13.

Chapter 2: "Performing the Rite of Marriage: Agency, Identity, and Ideology." *Proceedings of the North American Academy of Liturgy* 24 (2012) 93–105.

Chapter 3: "Holy Communion as Public Act: Ethics and Liturgical Participation." *Studia Liturgica* 41:1 (2011) 31–46.

Chapter 4: "Sign of Reconciliation and Conversion? Differing Views of Power—Ecclesial, Sacramental, and Anthropological—Among Hierarchy and Laity." *Theological Studies* 75:3 (2014) 585–612.

Chapter 5 is adapted from Part I and Conclusion in: Bordeyne, Philippe, and Bruce T. Morrill, "Baptism and Identity Formation: Convergences in Ritual and Ethical Perspectives: A Dialogue." *Studia Liturgica* 42 (2012) 154–75.

Chapter 6: "Liturgy, Ethics, and Politics: Constructive Inquiry into the Traditional Notion of Participation in Mystery." In *Mediating Mysteries, Understanding Liturgies: On Bridging the Gap Between Liturgy and Systematic Theology*, edited by Joris Geldhof, 187–206. Bibliotheca Ephemeridum Theologicarum Lovaniensium 278. Leuven: Peeters, 2015.

Chapter 7: "Pursuing the Intrinsic Relationship Between Liturgy and Ethics: Practical-Theological Promise in Poverty of Spirit." *Acta Universitatis Carolinae Theologica* 10:1 (2020) 77–98.

Chapter 8: "Sacramental Liturgy as Negotiation of Power, Human and Divine." In *Liturgy + Power*, edited by Brian P. Flanagan and Johann M. Vento, 3–21. College Theology Society Annual Volume 62. Maryknoll, NY: Orbis, 2017.

In addition to the above publishing opportunities, I benefited from numerous colleagues' speaking invitations, providing stimuli crucial to the development of my writings. Thus, a word of thanks and warm esteem to: Pierre Bordeyne, Institut Catholique de Paris, for inviting my address at the retirement colloquium for Louis-Marie Chauvet (2008); the Council of Societas Liturgica, for inviting my plenary co-address to the 23rd Congress (2011); Benedikt Kranemann, Universität Erfurt, for inviting my presentation to the Laien leiten Liturgie Conference (2011); Susan Ross, vice-president, for inviting my opening plenary address to the 67th Annual Convention of the Catholic Theological Society of America (2012); Joris Geldhof, Katholieke Universiteit Leuven, for inviting my plenary address to the 9th Leuven Encounters in Systematic Theology (2013); Claudio Burgaleta, SJ, Fordham University, for inviting me to hold the Loyola Chair, with its public lectures (2015); Victoria Tufano, Steven Janco, and Anthony Ruff, co-chairs, for inviting my plenary address to the Catholic Academy of Liturgy (2016); Brian Flanagan and Johann Vento, co-chairs, for inviting my opening plenary address to 62nd Annual Meeting of the College Theology Society (2016); Siobhan Garrigan, Head of School, for inviting my public lecture in the School of Religion, Trinity College Dublin (2017); as well as conveners and/or peer-reviewers of topical sessions and seminars at the annual meetings and congresses of the Catholic Theological Society of America, the North American Academy of Liturgy, and the Societas Liturgica.

Bruce T. Morrill, SJ
December 31, 2020
Seventh Day in the Octave of Christmas

Introduction

THEOLOGY THAT THINKS AND writes about the church's sacramental worship, its liturgy, is profitable only if it steadily attends in some direct way both to the actual practice of the church assembled in prayer and to the biblical-traditional content of the faith celebrated. What most fundamentally characterizes that faith, in Scripture and tradition, is the inextricable joining of God's glory to people's salvation, to theirs and the world's sanctification.

Sanctification, a most practical matter, is the key to Christian *liturgy* and ethics,[1] a concrete way of living out the divine love with which God's Spirit graces creation. Christianity has inherited from God's irreversible covenant with the Israelites the revelation of God's having wedded God's honor to the people's living in holiness, thereby making their entire lives the worship of God. "The Lord spoke to Moses, saying: Speak to all the congregation of the people of Israel and say to them: You shall be holy, for I the Lord your God am holy" (Lev 19:1–2). So opens an entire chapter of the Torah uniting ritual holiness to moral and social-ethical holiness, and all of that together as revelatory of holiness's divine source. Likewise follows one of the earliest instructions to those being baptized in the Christian faith: "[A]s he who called you is holy, be holy yourselves in all your conduct; for it is written, 'You shall be holy for I am holy'" (1 Pet 1:15–16).

Liturgical words and gestures proclaiming divine glory are empty, even potentially hazardous to both worshipers and the social world they inhabit, if practiced in isolation from the joys and hopes, griefs and anguish

---

1. For this axiom of my entire theological project, see Morrill, *Anamnesis*, 95–98; and Morrill, *Divine Worship*, 7–9. For a recent, related argument focused on holiness, see Geldhof, *Liturgy*, 72–74.

of fellow humans, especially the poor,[2] amidst "Our Common Home."[3] The work of the church's liturgical worship[4] is thereby at once sacramental and prophetic: sacramental because symbolically revealing God's saving presence and action in embodied lives, and prophetic because Christians continuously need their thoughts and actions (re)oriented to the divine imagination for the world.[5]

If God's creating, redeeming, sustaining love is eternally consistent, nonetheless, humanity's lives of ritual and ethical worship, of glorifying God, are subject to the changing conditions of times and places. History and narrative are thereby essential to any theology seeking to serve the practical living of the faith. The following eight chapters present one effort at attending to the dynamics of liturgy and ethics, specifically within the Roman Catholic tradition in its contemporary US context, but always in an ecumenically open spirit.

Part II, "Sacramental Rites in Performative Perspective," approaches sacramental liturgy from the side of popular (lay and ordained) perceptions and practices, using a method of description (historical and contemporary accounts) and analysis (theological judgments and proposals grounded in Scripture, tradition, and critical scholarship). An unapologetic degree of controversy (for which the social-scientific term is "contestation") characterizes the chapters' approaches to marriage, Holy Communion, and penance in US Catholicism. Marriage takes the lead, due to the pointed degree to which all parties involved tend to be highly invested in the sacramental rite's execution, yet with divergent and at times conflicting priorities. Part III, "Liturgy and Ethics, Scripture and Tradition," while not neglecting contemporary conditions of sacramental-liturgical practice, takes a more normative approach, theologically constructing the relationship between liturgical worship and life-ethic on the basis of strategically identified loci in the catholic (not just narrowly Roman Catholic) tradition: baptismal initiation and ongoing renewal, participation in mystery, and poverty of spirit. Here, baptism and Eucharist (sacraments fundamental across churches and liturgical-ecclesial bodies) take the lead, as might traditionally be expected. Still, for all three chapters, tradition proves vital only if biblically grounded yet actively attuned to time and place.

2. See Paul VI, *Gaudium et Spes*, no. 1.

3. Francis, *Laudato Si'*, nos. 48–52, 233–37.

4. The root of the Greek word *leitourgia* being *ergon*, "a work."

5. The gospel language for that being the kingdom or reign of God.

Introduction

The opening and concluding sections frame the book with its most concertedly methodological chapters, surveying and integrating theological, philosophical, and social-scientific currents that inform the concrete approaches taken in the six main chapters. Should readers find themselves bogged down in chapter 1's methodological review of modern sacramental-liturgical theology, along with its constructive proposals, one could leave it aside and dig into the narrative-descriptive chapters in Part II. The bevy of issues raised in those chapters will hopefully motivate exploration of the relevant biblical-traditional resources in Part III. The concluding chapter revisits, albeit from a different angle, some of the key points in the opening one, such that readers, having worked through the content of the two main parts of the book, might find themselves more attuned to engaging with the author in questions of theory and academic method. Readers will still find, nonetheless, that even that concluding chapter rounds out its arguments with one more practical, pastoral-liturgical example. To echo the great hermeneutical philosopher Paul Ricoeur, the symbol gives rise to thought, just as thought must surely return to the symbol.

Part I

Theorizing Practice

1

Contemporary
Sacramental-Liturgical Theology
The Dialectic of Meaning and Performance[1]

A Half-Century's Review

WITH APOLOGIES FOR SUCH a prosaic entrée to this presentation, I wish
to begin by commenting on its title—specifically, first, on my placing the
term *Dialectic* at the center of the title for the opening plenary address of an
annual meeting thematically focused on *Sacrament(s)*. If you would allow
me a bit of conjecture, I could imagine that in the period surrounding the
Second Vatican Council—say, the 1950s through early 1970s—theologians
might well have mused over the joining of sacrament and dialectic as a sort
of category mistake. After all, had not the methodological boundary lines
among classroom theologians achieved a certain fixity opposing dialectical
thought from sacramental and/or analogical imagination? While such sophisticated analysis of the two paradigms' paragons, Barth and Rahner, as

---

1. The text of this chapter first served as the opening plenary address for the 67th
Annual Convention of the Catholic Theological Society of America (June 2012). This
accounts for both the style of delivery and discussion of technical concepts presumably
familiar to the audience. The last paragraphs of the chapter replace an original discussion of marriage, replacing that with a transition into that very topic as the focus of the
ensuing chapter 2.

performed by David Tracy[2] would come to find more in common between each Karl's utterly modern project than seemed evident to their average readers, still, conventional thought among American Catholic theologians and popular writers has asserted the analogical or sacramental imagination as a defining characteristic of Catholic thought and practice.[3]

But that reference to practice leads to a second comment about my title for a presentation whose charge is to assess, at least in this American context, the state of the sacramental-theological question fifty years after the beginning of Vatican II. For there has been a dialectical tension concerning the subject matter of sacrament itself within the American Catholic theological academy during the past five decades. Put bluntly, although it is now a waning phenomenon in this new century, over the better part of the period after Vatican II systematic theologians, perhaps more on doctoral faculties, tended to consider liturgical theology an inferior intellectual enterprise, at times even to the point of scorn.

There, I've said it! And I say it as one whose academic-theological career earlier found itself in the crosshairs of such attitudes, sometimes articulated, other times thinly veiled. The tension—perhaps dialectical— has been primarily due to systematic theologians' pride in pursuing pure thought, doctrine founded upon argument (rather than mystery), *fides quaerens intellectum*, but a faith identified first and foremost with concepts. In the late 1970s, Johann Baptist Metz attacked this notion of faith as an idea, as some transcendental apperception, countering that faith is fundamentally a praxis, a praxis of mysticism and ethics whose irreducible elements of memory, narrative, and solidarity comprise the contours of a "practical fundamental theology."[4] Still, among systematic theologians, not only much of the old guard, but now, I fear, even some of the new, political and liberation theologies' goal that praxis-thinking fundamentally pervade

---

2. See Tracy, *Analogical Imagination*, 107, 412, 416–18.

3. See McBrien, *Catholicism*, 15–17, 1196–1200; Himes, "Finding God," 91–92, 99–101; and Greeley, *Catholic Imagination*, especially 1–22.

4. "The universality of the offer of salvation in Christianity does not have the character of a transcendental concept of universality or a concept drawn out from universal history. . . . In christological terms this means that the salvation 'for everyone' that is grounded in Christ does not become universal by means of an idea, but by means of the intelligible power of a praxis: the praxis of discipleship. This intelligibility of Christianity cannot be conveyed in a purely speculative way, but narratively." Metz, *Faith in History*, 28–30, 71–74, 84; see also Morrill, *Anamnesis*, 74–75, 189–91.

academic theology found an uneven reception.[5] Rather, Metz's work, for example, largely stands as another concept to study, another method, among others, to consider, perhaps for which to be responsible on a doctoral comps reading list. While the reasons for this resistance to prioritizing praxis in thought no doubt rest in ideological causes situated in each of theology's three publics—academy, church, and society[6]—my task here, of course, is to address what about sacraments seemed (perhaps still seems) so threatening to "real" or "serious" systematic theology.

It would not seem too risky to suggest that one of the primary reasons the subject matter of sacraments and liturgy would strike the men who received their theological doctorates in the 1950s through the 1970s as minimally worthy of concerted theological discipline was the fact that in their seminary training the sacraments were the subject of canon law in a doctrinal theology course, with some further Thomistic treatment through the tenets of transubstantiation, matter, and form.[7] Sacraments were effectively a matter of practical power, that is, clerical power, which bore with it the responsibility for teaching their validity, whether catechetically to Catholics or apologetically to others.[8] The rites themselves, on the other hand and in practical detail, comprised the domain of liturgists characteristically consumed with rubrics, often combining legal precision with imposed aesthetics, such that the old joke about the difference between a liturgist and a terrorist[9] could persist at least into my own time in the 1990s.

Be that as it may, the methodological tension over the relevance, if not necessity, of actual (ritual) practice to academic theology even persisted

---

5. Thus, Gutiérrez: "[T]he theology of liberation proposes for us not so much a new theme for reflection as a *new way* to do theology." Gutiérrez, *Theology of Liberation*, 12.

6. On these "Three Publics of Theology," see Tracy, *Analogical Imagination*, 3–28.

7. French pastoral theologian Philippe Barras articulates the outcome of such seminary training by distinguishing between "a 'nonliturgical' sacramental praxis, understood as a deployment of a catechetical arsenal on the occasion of sacramental administration, and a sacramental pastoral praxis that as a part of the pastoral liturgy has for its objective to open and inscribe the way of Christian existence in its relationship to God, initiated or marked by the event that constitutes the liturgical celebration of the sacrament." Barras, "Sacramental Theology," 89.

8. During this very time period, on the other hand, as James F. White recounts, began "the intentional training of liturgy professors for seminaries," first at the Institut Catholique de Paris in the 1950s, and then the Sant' Anselmo in Rome and Notre Dame in the USA in the 1960s. See White, "Forum," 439.

9. What's the difference between a terrorist and a liturgist? With a terrorist you can at least negotiate sometimes.

among those specializing in sacraments. The experiential turn in American Catholic sacramental theology took its cues from the early Schillebeeckx and consistent Rahner, focusing phenomenologically on human-developmental qualities of encounter and event but still not attending closely to ritual texts and dynamics. In a 1984 issue of the journal *Worship*, liturgical theologian John Baldovin concluded his appreciative review of two then-newly published books on the sacraments, including Bernard Cooke's still widely read *Sacraments & Sacramentality*, as follows:

> My fundamental criticism of both books will not seem strange coming from a student of the liturgy. I was unable to find in either text a single quotation or reference to the reformed rites of the Roman Catholic Church or to their general instructions or *praenotanda*. Until sacramental theology begins to take the actual celebration of the sacraments seriously as a starting point it will be guilty of the accusation leveled by Louis Boyer against eucharistic theology twenty years ago: here we have theologies about the sacraments, not theologies of the sacraments.[10]

If sacramental theology as a systematic effort was predominantly phenomenological in pursuing how and why sacraments are anthropologically basic and ecclesiologically essential,[11] liturgical theology addressed the rites largely through historical and textual work. In a 1994 essay, Methodist liturgical scholar James White noted that of the fifty-four PhDs the liturgical studies program at Notre Dame had produced since its founding in 1966,

10. Baldovin, "Review," 550–51. In the closing paragraph of his preface to that book's second edition, Cooke offers: "For a time I played with the idea of a much lengthier revision, one that would treat at greater length the various sacramental liturgies. However, I rejected this approach because I did not want to distract from the main purpose of this book: to draw attention to the *basic sacramentality of Christian life* that grounds the meaning and effectiveness of the liturgical rituals. Understanding, appreciating, and living out this sacramentality is, I believe, the most important element in the development of Christian spirituality." Cooke, *Sacraments*, vi.

11. Another systematic project, this time based on a Lonerganian concept of conversion, was Donald Gelpi's two-volume *Committed Worship* (1993), for which Notre Dame liturgical historian Maxwell E. Johnson opened his review: "[A] largely successful attempt to articulate a 'foundational theology' of conversion in relation to the current Roman Catholic reformed rites of the seven sacraments. Readers expecting a historical-critical treatment of sacramental theology or a detailed theological analysis of the texts of the current rites, however, should be forewarned." Further down, Johnson avers: "My major problem with this work does not center on his theology of conversion *per se* but on the application of this theology as necessarily foundational to the sacraments themselves in the remaining sections [of the two volumes]." Johnson, "Review," 465–66.

all but five were "historical in subject matter."[12] White's comments point to two distinctions about twentieth-century liturgical studies in general contrast to Catholic sacramental theology; namely, its ecumenical commitments and text-centered historical work.

Those salient features of liturgical theology had some methodological problems of their own. The laudable ecumenical impulses of liturgical scholars across the gamut of Western mainstream denominations, all of whom held the Second Vatican Council's Constitution on the Sacred Liturgy as their charter document,[13] often consorted with the modern tendency to construct a master narrative based on the myth of some indubitable historical origin. With sincere if not passionate pastoral agendas, and often as the officially deputed authors of the revised rites for their respective ecclesial communions, liturgical scholars sought common, normative grounds in the primordial content and forms of Christians rites, pursued through quests for the *Urtext* of each liturgical unit. In this, as in every case, history was hermeneutics: interpreting texts to support arguments for how liturgical and sacramental rites should now be constructed so as to generate genuine renewal within and among Christian communities. By the turn of the twenty-first century, Notre Dame professor and prominent Anglican scholar of early Christian liturgy Paul Bradshaw called to account all those colleagues who had been "lumping" ancient sources into single normative patterns for their grossly ignoring the constant significant differences of detail in the texts.[14] There persisted a troubling phenomenon: Too often, if not so much in print as in local practice, whatever contemporary pastoral applications liturgists wanted to assert arose from their historical persnicketiness, thus advancing not only the liturgical terrorist syndrome but also the charge from systematic theologians, again not in print but in conversations at conferences (I can attest), that the liturgists lacked the philosophical firepower to justify their normative claims.

Lest I paint too polemical a polarized picture, however, I should acknowledge that certainly by the 1980s the better systematic theologians had come to embrace historical studies as essential to crafting re-articulations

12. White, "Forum," 443.

13. Historian Bryan Spinks explains: "[The] *Constitution on the Sacred Liturgy* . . . acted as an instant catalyst in sparking unprecedented liturgical experimentation and revision throughout Anglicanism and in most major Protestant churches." Spinks, "Anglicans and Dissenters," 526. See also Schmidt-Lauber, "Lutheran Tradition," 396, 415; and Tucker, "North America," 625–26.

14. See Bradshaw, *Search for the Origins*, 6–20.

of the faith adequate to contemporary circumstances. On the topic of sacraments, that methodological shift was evident in Bernard Cooke's monumental work on ministry, for which the straightforward subtitle was simply, *History and Theology*.[15] During the remaining two decades of the twentieth century, David Power produced several books on liturgy and sacraments that integrated history and hermeneutics so as to construct systematic arguments for what renewed ecclesial practice could be in late-modern and globalized contexts.[16] Meanwhile, his Catholic University colleague Mary Collins had already produced a number of compelling articles using anthropology and ritual theories not only to substantiate constructive proposals but also to deconstruct the clerical power retarding truly enculturated, liberating reforms in sacramental celebration. Her 1979 essay on the history of and ideology entailed in official restrictions on the making and handling of the eucharistic bread remains a *tour de force* both in content and methodology.[17] Other notable women's contributions line up rather more along the systematic and liturgical theological divide. In 2001, Susan Ross's *Extravagant Affections* integrated systematic, psychoanalytic, and ethical theories to craft an enduring and ecumenically influential feminist sacramental theology, while Teresa Berger's contributions have come through more historical and liturgical study with a disarming attentiveness to not only women's but also wider popular religious and devotional experiences.[18]

Power and Collins, as well as Margaret Kelleher, Edward Kilmartin, and Robert Daly (with apologies for my leaving others out) were active leaders of seminars and ongoing work groups in both the North American Academy of Liturgy and the Catholic Theological Society of America. Through their productive and creative scholarship, the regular session they organized at the annual CTSA meeting by the 1990s was called the "Sacramental and Liturgical Theology Group," a title indicating the felicitous convergence that the dialectics of theory and practice in the two decreasingly polarized sub-disciplines were attaining. The doctrinal principle from

15. See Cooke, *Ministry to Word and Sacrament*.

16. See Power, *Unsearchable Riches*; Power, *Sacrifice We Offer*; Power, *Eucharistic Mystery*; and Power, *Sacrament*.

17. See Collins, "Critical Questions."

18. See Ross, *Extravagant Affections*. See also Berger, *Women's Ways*; Berger, *Gender Differences*; and her numerous articles in *Studia Liturgica* and *Worship*.

Vatican II[19] common to sacramental and liturgical theologies (European and American) was the abandonment of scholasticism's treatment of sacraments as following from a christology of incarnation to situating the Church's sacramental rites in the paschal mystery, a concept biblically and patristically rooted in theological reflection on the Church's ritual celebrations of the mystery of faith that came through two lines of development: one emphasizing the sacraments as participation in the definitive salvific event of Jesus' death and resurrection, the other emphasizing sacraments as immersing believers in the work of salvation Christ's death and resurrection continues to realize in their lives and, ultimately, for the life of the world.

Still to be overcome, nonetheless, or at least ever vigilantly checked, in sacramental-liturgical theology is the pernicious problem of textual positivism. From its inception circa 1870, liturgical theology tended to be a study of ritual books—their orations, rubrics, and commentaries—with an often-misguided presumption that an analysis of the texts reveals not only the meaning of the rites in themselves but the impact they had on those who celebrated them. While that impressive corpus of work has undeniably been fruitful, its text-bound methods have proven ultimately insufficient. The unfortunate corollary to this mindset has been the naïve conviction that contemporary liturgical renewal is a matter of getting the words of texts somehow exactly correct, with the expectation that the clergy's pronouncing them and the people's hearing them will somehow automatically and intellectually instill a proper theology, even a practical one, at that.[20] Thus, Jewish liturgical theologian Lawrence Hoffman in 1987 and, learning from him, Monsignor Kevin Irwin in 1994 made significant contributions by writing books arguing for how context shapes text, and vice versa.[21] Meanwhile, in 1990, Bernard Cooke attempted a survey of Christian symbol broadly conceived through the major epochs of Christian history so as to argue for how the primordial Christian encounter with the risen Christ was impeded by ecclesial, philosophical, and ritual structures, while raising counter examples of popular religious movements and literary works he argued promoted Christians' recognition of the triune God's presence and

19. See Paul VI, *Sacrosanctum Concilium*, no. 5.

20. In his prodigious and detailed work (numbering more than six hundred essays and some twenty books) the eminent Jesuit liturgical historian Robert F. Taft, SJ, never tired of pointing out the foolishness in anachronistically approaching texts, while often skewering the ideological biases of those so inclined.

21. See Hoffman, *Beyond the Text*; and Irwin, *Context and Text*.

action in their lives.[22] Cooke's method attended to an impressive range of literature replete with suggestive insights, yet his remaining inattentiveness to liturgical details and his sweeping systematic-philosophical assumptions left that work open to criticism from various angles.

More attentive to context *and* liturgical text were David Power, in his aforementioned several books, and Nathan Mitchell in his bimonthly "Amen Corner" in the journal *Worship*. Power proved intrepid in his attention to the mutual influence of ecclesial and social cultures upon the medieval and then counter-reformation sacramental rites and theologies so as to argue for contemporary theology's need to recover critically the biblical, narrative content of the faith amidst what he unflinchingly described as the "ruins" of a post-Tridentine piety and theology now impotent amidst the likewise ruined promises of modernity.[23] Mitchell's analysis of whatever liturgical documents, practices, and spiritualities he considered relevant or even pressing in a given installment of his bimonthly column, he consistently executed with consideration of the changing social and personal-subjective conditions of post-modernity, approaching his material with an open mind while turning an iconoclastic eye on official Roman Catholic liturgical regulations, practices, and theologies. A distinctive influence on both men's work was Louis-Marie Chauvet, who, during his several decades as a fundamental theologian at the Institut Catholique de Paris, produced what is arguably the most influential book in sacramental-liturgical theology since the early contributions of Rahner and Schillebeeckx. Chauvet continues to add to the scores of articles he has published, primarily in the thrice-yearly *La Maison-Dieu*, addressing each and all of the rites in pastoral-liturgical detail.

The French original of Chauvet's magnum opus, *Symbol and Sacrament*, came out in 1987, coincidentally the same year as Hoffman's *Beyond the Text*, while the American-English translation appeared, likewise coincidentally, a year after Irwin's *Context and Text*. Chauvet's sacramental theology, while regularly attentive to historical texts and practices, is a philosophical interpretation of how God's having taken up and saved the human condition in the life, death, and resurrection of Jesus becomes real in the lives of those baptized into that same paschal mystery.[24] The

22. See Cooke, *Distancing*, 143–48, 172–84.

23. See Power, *Eucharistic Mystery*, vii, 13; and Power, *Sacrament*, 18.

24. My rehearsal of Chauvet's theology in this and the next paragraph is taken directly from my part of the introduction to his Festschrift. See Morrill, "Building," xvi, xxi–xii.

Church's symbolic order of Scripture, sacrament, and ethics makes of the human subject's historically and culturally mediated project of knowledge, gratitude, and ethics a sacrament—an embodied revelation—of the reign of God, the salvation of human beings. What keeps this way of life explicitly Christian is ongoing balance between these three constitutive poles of the practice of faith. Only by submitting to the resistance of reality revealed in each dimension's juxtaposition to the others do believers continue to give themselves over to the otherness, the presence-in-absence of the God of Jesus. At the heart of Chauvet's fundamental sacramental theology is his insistence that the sacraments of the Church are practices of *faith*, with faith being "the assent to a loss,"[25] a continuous letting go of our projections of what we imagine God should be like, so that the totally other yet lovingly near God revealed in the crucified and resurrected Christ might really be present to us in our lived experience.

The corporality of the practice of the sacraments, precisely as language-laden, communal acts of symbolic mediation, is what makes their celebration so essential to knowing and living the Christ proclaimed in Scripture. Participation in sacramental liturgy, as an ecclesial body given over to the Word in both Scripture and symbolic (sacramental) gestures that inscribe that divine Word on our persons, delivers us from the human tendency to imagine that there should be no distance, no gap, no otherness between ourselves and the fullness of God. The members of a liturgical assembly bring precisely their bodies to the celebration, their daily action (ethics) as persons engaged in the social and cosmic bodiliness of the human story being written in history. By participating in the traditional body of the Church's sacramental worship, we submit to the mystery of God revealed in the crucified and resurrected Jesus, a God who comes to us in and through the shared bodily medium of our human knowing, suffering, and loving. Thus does the God of Jesus become really present to our lives, even as that sacramental ecclesial presence always recedes in its coming, sending us in the Spirit to discover the Word as living and active in us and in our world.

Chauvet thus pressed for sacraments as presence of the absent one, of faith as an assent to a loss (*un manque*, "a lack"), opening the necessity of mediation in all its human bodily complexity—natural, social, and traditional. Systematic theologian Jean-Louis Souletie has provided an

25. Chauvet, *Sacraments*, 39.

assessment of the necessity for theology's greater engagement with the social sciences that follows from Chauvet's original contribution:

> The status of truth changes in this approach. If truth always exceeds the discourse that one has about it, it seemed to Chauvet that it should verify itself through the passage of these long mediations by which the human comes about. The theological task is obvious. Ritual mediation is not an anecdote. It gives access to the truth of faith and participates in the construction of the believing subject in its linguistic, material, psychic and political ambiguities. The social sciences have no other ambition here than to eradicate illusions of immediacy, which lodge themselves in these corporal mediations where the human and believer become. But positively they will help sacramental theology to think about itself further in the register of grace understood as "God who makes profitable the symbolic field that is the believing subject."[26]

Souletie notes criticisms of Chauvet on the question of whether the anthropological priority of the symbolic comes at the cost of the proper theological efficacy of the sacramental,[27] a concern resonant with Power's questioning earlier whether Chauvet's dismissal of ontology and reliance on gift-exchange theory is theologically sufficient to counter the mythical language of sacrifice that continues to distort theologies and practices of the Eucharist.[28] Given the contested and, indeed, declining state of active membership and regular liturgical participation in early twenty-first century American Catholicism, however, my own concerns are less with the metaphysical and more in league with Chauvet's fundamental-practical agenda, prioritizing pastoral efficacy over clerical-hierarchical-institutional security in the still-unrealized reform and renewal of sacraments and liturgy. What Souletie and Chauvet call social science, I shall now in a shorter second half of this presentation enlist in the burgeoning genres of ritual theory and performance studies, as resources for more adequately accessing in actual, contextual liturgical practices the dialectics of meaning and performance in American Catholic rites today.

---

26. Souletie, "Social Sciences," 195. Souletie quotes Chauvet, "Quand la théologie," 408.

27. See Souletie, "Social Sciences," 195–96.

28. See Morrill, "Les raisons," 180; and Power, *Eucharistic Mystery*, 324–25.

A Constructive Way Forward

Did you note what Souletie had to say about truth? The status of truth changes in a theology that locates truth in the actual existence of Christian corporal and corporate practices of word, sacrament, and ethics, that situates truth in a church who in its members knows how permeable are its boundaries in a world that ultimately belongs to God. Such a theology cannot but have devastating implications for those who equate the understanding of faith with totalizing control over bodies—bodies of knowledge, bodies at worship, bodies that love and sin. The symbolic-sacramental relocation of truth in a faith practiced and known in history and society swings its axe at the base of hierarchical ladders propped up inside defensive walls academic and clerical, transcendentally idealist and ecclesially triumphalist. Seeking the truth theologically in "the long mediations" of ritualized and ethical bodies—which, in all their ambiguities, are the only human bodies we have or can know—methodologically requires constant narrative descriptions and rigorous intellectual analyses if sacramental-liturgical theology is to contribute to not only the academy but also church and society in what can only be described as a time of crisis at the interface of those three publics in twenty-first century Catholicism. Sacramental-liturgical theology can make its proper, original contribution at this moment, I would propose, precisely by "eradicating illusions of immediacy" with the help of such social-scientific disciplines as ritual and performance studies. To do so requires no small measure of courage, for it is to go against the grain of the most rigorously held (because insufficiently critical) assumptions of modern thought, both religious and secular. Allow me to explore and, hopefully, to explain.

Perhaps the primary reason many Catholic academics and ecclesiastical authorities have been wary or dismissive toward sacramental and/or liturgical theology is because they know, even if only subconsciously, that ritual is fluid with time and corporality, that "[r]itual's repeated, performative, and antidiscursive nature," as social scientists Adam Seligman and associates argue, "provides a critical way of dealing with rather than overcoming, the eternal contradiction and ambiguity of human existence."[29] Seligman and associates place *ritual* (broadly conceived) at one end of the human continuum for "framing experience, action, and understanding," while at the other end (and in ongoing tension) is what they call *sincerity*,

29. Seligman et al., *Ritual*, 129–30.

which values individual decision and the exercise of the will, the workings of which "are singular, unique, discursive, and indicative to the highest degree."[30] Human ritual negotiates ambiguity without completely resolving it, as would, in contrast, a discursive (that is, sincere) explanation. Indeed, the ambiguity that haunts all boundaries in life—physical, social, and traditional—is the very reason for ritualizing. Ritual is the way we humans hold the many irresolvable ambivalences of life in a *both-and* tension that orients and, with repetition, reorients a people's identity and agency amidst the ambiguities of interpersonal, social, and cosmic relations, as well as through the changes in the individual life cycle—with death always looming around the edges. Attention to such human activity does not lend itself well to the pursuit of certitude through pure argument in the academy, nor to apodictic assertions about the singular proper execution of a given rite and its meaning in the sanctuary.

Perhaps, then, the ambiguity inherent to actual ritual performances as practices in particular contexts is likewise the reason for the textual positivism that so long plagued liturgical theology and, I'm sorry to observe, persists in certain theologians' expectations that, for example, getting the language of the eucharistic prayer exactly, conceptually right, and then the people—clergy and laity—thoroughly educated in its meaning, is a promising theoretical (theological) and practical (pastoral) plan. This points to the fundamental error pervading a half-millennium of Western Christian theologies (Protestant and Catholic) steeped in modern academic thought; namely, the assumption that ritual is merely expressive of meaning, a dualistic notion dismissive of the bodily nature of ritual—and thus of humanity, for that matter.[31] Such bias, following from Enlightenment thought, misses what the Seligman group insightfully argue is ritual's most profound power: Participation in its repetitive, rhythmic structure creates a "shared subjunctive," a moment of experiential knowledge of the world as what it could or should be, forming participants to appropriate such a worldview, along with their roles therein. As a corporate, shared human exercise, the performed symbolism of a ritual affects the thought and sensibilities of its participants, such that "the medium is very much the message."[32] For academic liturgical

30. Seligman et al., *Ritual*, 7, 118; see also 41–47.

31. Catherine Bell levels this critique against modern philosophical and social-scientific methodologies in terms of a privileged dichotomy of thought over action. See Bell, *Ritual Theory*, 48–49.

32. Seligman et al., *Ritual*, 10.

theology to provide original, constructive insight (*intellectum*) into the ritual praxis of the faith requires constant renunciation of textual positivism. In its stead comes the daunting challenge of developing methodologies to account for what is happening in the complex bodily, multivalent physical, social, and traditional dimensions of the sacraments in context.

As social theorists, Seligman and associates write out of a sense of practical concern, if not urgency, for our contemporary global society. Persuasive is their argument that modern blinders to the power exercised in the pervasive ritual activities—political, religious, commercial, and interpersonal—that variably unite and divide, often violently, peoples on local, national, and international scales prevent accessing key resources for identifying and helping scenarios of tension and conflict. For my part, I think there is much to be gained in adopting their insightful arguments for the social body that is the church. For we have witnessed over the past several decades within Roman Catholicism, as well as other "mainstream" ecclesial bodies, the so-called "liturgy wars," genuine power struggles over the extent to which the official rites—their words, symbols, gestures, and ministerial actors—adequately serve the needs of the majority of believers acculturated to the modern priorities of self-expression and personal authenticity. While Catholicism, with its readily identifiable sacramental-ritual system, abstractly considered, may seem not to be so affected by the modern diminution of ritual in the individual subject's sincere quest for meaning, the simplistic touting of the so-called Catholic or sacramental imagination at this point in American history is prone to ignoring the increasingly precipitous decline in levels of participation in sacramental rites the American church has been witnessing in its members for decades.

While decreased regular Sunday Mass attendance has garnered attention in its recent acceleration, the fact is that the practice of the Rite of Penance collapsed in the late 1960s and has not recovered or found—better said, been officially *allowed* to find—a new way forward.[33] I continue to state the obvious in noting that the sacrament of orders (the priesthood) has likewise plunged in actual participation, but we should not ignore the startling degree to which the marked decline in marriages across the American population is no less statistically evident for Roman Catholics. These significant changes in ritual-symbolic practice are not all simply due to the controlling agenda of the Church hierarchy, as liberals might contend, nor

---

33. For a full account and assessment of this recent ecclesial history, see chapter 4, below.

simply to the decadence of techno-commercial culture, as might the conservatives. No, the situation is far more complex precisely due to the fact that the liturgical rites, as ritual practices, are not simply expressive of ideas already decided and/or social roles statically set.[34] Social-scientific help is needed for a practical-theological anthropology adequate to the demanding questions and problems, but also promise, for sacramental-liturgical praxis.

Here the highly influential work of the late Catherine Bell is pertinent. In her widely read *Ritual Theory, Ritual Practice*, Bell summarized what theorists are arguing against as they press to make the particular activity of a given ritual understandable (to use a phrase more recently coined by Don Handelman[35]) *in its own right*:

> [I]t is a major reversal of traditional theory to hypothesize that ritual activity is not the "instrument" of more basic purposes, such as power, politics, or social control, which are usually seen as existing before or outside the activities of the rite. It puts interpretive analysis on a new footing to suggest that ritual practices are themselves the very production and negotiation of power relations.

In this alternate theoretical position "ritualization as a strategic mode of practice produces nuanced relationships of power, relationships characterized by acceptance and resistance, negotiated appropriation and redemptive reinterpretation of the hegemonic order."[36] The following, first major part of the present book takes full advantage of Bell's critical insight that, in the end (if not beginning!), ritual is better understood not as a static thing but, rather, an activity, such that scholarly analysis better describes and analyzes events of people "ritualizing"[37] strategically in social-historical contexts. The context is late-modern US Catholicism, and the ritualizing, studied in three successive chapters, entails the sacraments of marriage, Eucharist, and penance.

The chapters comprising Part II, "Sacramental Rites in Performative Perspective," pursue the thesis that Christian sacraments, specifically within the Roman Catholic tradition, do not somehow exist noetically and need only be expressed ritually. I present them as cases that might help

34. For a narrative account of one pastoral example, opening into theological analysis, see Morrill, *Encountering Christ*, 38–45.

35. See Handelman, "Introduction," 1–32.

36. Bell, *Ritual Theory*, 196.

37. Bell, *Ritual Theory*, 7–8.

wider pastoral and practical-theological audiences appreciate what is at stake as current sacramental-liturgical theologians, such as myself, pursue the seemingly asymptotic implications of the twentieth-century liturgical-theological consensus that the actual celebrations of rites comprise the "primary theology"[38] of the church. This is to try to get at something of Christian faith's "long mediations" of truth with a humility hopefully approximating that of Chauvet, not just in the immediate moment but, through the hard work of publication, for the benefit of generations to come—that is, assuming (hoping!) there will be in future centuries people interested in tracing the longer arc of truth's mediation in the ongoing praxis of Catholic and Christian traditions. This is to understand the scholarly theological vocation as providing a record of both the theory and practice of the sacramental rites of the church in this volatile period of its history, and this in the register not of mere observation but of committed ecclesial participation.

What distinguishes the work as theological, in comparison and in contrast to others engaged in what anthropologist Ronald Grimes broadly identifies as "ritual criticism,"[39] are the particular criteria used to make judgments about the efficaciousness of the church's liturgical practices, as well as about the official and academic practices of writing thereon. Given the present and increasingly polarized ecclesial situation, the clerical assertions of control, the emptying pews, the youthful and even middle-aged alienation of the faithful, the hegemony of market- and technologically driven individualism to the detriment of the commonweal, the task is for sacramental-liturgical theology to provide church and academy perceptive, descriptive work to help articulate what is going on. The task likewise entails analytical work to venture theological judgments about what the church's ongoing sacramental-liturgical tradition has to offer, as well as how that ritual treasury is being profitably exploited or tragically squandered in practice. This surely is not to surrender the theological task to religious studies. What marks such work as theological, as it does Chauvet's, is the recourse to the biblical content of the faith as mediated through the mutually informing practices of word, sacrament, and ethics, studied scientifically in present contexts and with ongoing recourse to history and tradition, to traditions enacted historically.[40] And so, I conclude with a bow to truth

38. See Fagerberg, *Theologia Prima*, 39–45.

39. See Grimes, "Scholarly Contexts," 214–15.

40. My most sustained exercise of this method of liturgical theology may be found in my biblically, historically, social-scientifically, and ritually constructed theology of the Roman Catholic Church's current rites for the sick, dying, deceased, and mourners. See

as performatively known and practically lived in an ongoing dialectic of liturgy and ethics, for articulation of that tension may be a principal way for sacramental-liturgical theology to serve its publics, present and future.

Morrill, *Divine Worship*. For another (highly successful) example, see Belcher, *Efficacious Engagement*.

Part II

Sacramental Rites
in Performative Perspective

2

Marriage

Agency, Identity, and Ideology
in Ritual Performance

Theorizing Ritual: The Priority of Practice

THE QUESTION FOR THE liturgical scholar, whether theologian or "liturgiologist," to use Ronald Grimes's nomenclature,[1] is one of location among a variety of academic fields engaging ritual. Several decades ago, sacramental-liturgical theologian Mary Collins astutely questioned when her peers would not only study and apply ritual theories from the philosophical and social sciences but also begin to proffer their own theories and methods as viable with and, indeed, valuable to those other academic disciplines.[2] For his part, the anthropologist Grimes clearly places theologians and liturgiologists on equal footing with the whole host of other scholars interested in ritual, fully expecting to learn from what liturgical theologians have to offer by their ways of being ritual critics. Collins's wise and astute challenge, of course, entails the liturgical theologian's availing themselves of insights from theorists across the whole range of scientific disciplines.

What I hear in Collins's exhortation, as well as in Grimes's invitation, nonetheless, is the disqualification of any defensiveness or unnecessary

1. Grimes, "Scholarly Contexts," 214–15.
2. See Collins, "Church," 30–34.

apologetics on the part of the sacramental-liturgical theologian in his or her contextual practice of what Grimes broadly calls ritual criticism. Grimes essays a theory of the ritual critic as one who evaluates the efficaciousness of a particular ritual practice, doing so reflexively aware that any act of criticism is itself "judgment-laden," and thus "must systematically attend to the politics of critique." For both anthropologists and "religiologists" studying ritual, Grimes argues, "Criticism is inescapable, though one can minimize, disguise, or try to subdue it. There is no possibility of fully disengaging normative and critical intentions from descriptive ones."[3] My point at the outset, then, is to acknowledge both the flexibility in theory that the range of ritual studies affords and my own reflexivity as one type of ritual critic; namely, a sacramental-liturgical theologian and Roman Catholic priest, in the following consideration of the Rite of Marriage[4] in contemporary US Catholicism.

The Contemporary Rite of Marriage as Ideology in Practice

If ever there were a particular ceremony in Roman Catholicism demonstrative of how ritual does not simply express or symbolize a presumed, established, univocal religious ideology, it is the celebration of matrimony. In this present exercise of ritual criticism, I adopt Bell's rejections of the long-regnant modern "ideology-as-worldview perspective," with "its 'totalistic fallacy,' the assumption that a group is dominated by a single, holistic set of ideas, which acts as the cement for [a given] society."[5] The society in this case is the Roman Catholic Church in the USA, and the dominant class, the local clergy (priests and deacons) to whom the laity would be seen as the passively obliging underclass, with said clergy likewise viewed as obediently subservient to the official rites and ongoing directives (canonical and

---

3. Grimes, "Scholarly Contexts," 226, 216, 227.

4. In the time between the original publication of this chapter as a scholarly article in 2012 and its present, adapted form in this book, the US Conference of Catholic Bishops, in compliance with Vatican directives, replaced the prior Rite of Marriage (1969) with the Order for Celebrating Matrimony (2016). The new text (its Introduction and Rites) implements some revisions the Vatican had made to the official Latin edition, while also employing standards for all liturgical translations the Vatican had promulgated in 2011. In this present chapter, I have found it necessary, in the context of the narratives, still to refer to the then-current Rite of Marriage in places.

5. Bell, *Ritual Theory*, 188.

otherwise) issued by the Vatican hierarchy and executed by the bishops they appoint across the globe.

As I shall attempt to demonstrate in the following descriptive (narrative) and analytic (critical, theological) work, the actual ritualizing of the sacrament of marriage provides considerable evidence to support Bell's important conclusion that

> ideology is best understood as a strategy of power, a process whereby certain social practices or institutions are depicted to be "natural" and "right." While such a strategy implies the existence of a group or groups whose members stand to gain in some way by an acceptance of these practices, it also implies the existence of some form of opposition. Thus, ideologization may imply an unequal distribution of power, but it also indicates a greater distribution of power than would exist in relationships defined by sheer force. It is a strategy intimately connected with legitimation, discourse, and fairly high degrees of social complicity and maneuverability.[6]

To my mind, in Catholic (as well as Orthodox) Christianity, Bell's general (yet comprehensive) description of ideology functions under the title "tradition." Among and across the full range of practitioners of Catholicism (hierarchs and lower clerics, clergy and laity, generational cohorts, ethnic and national groups, social classes, genders, and more) the faithful vary in how they identify and prioritize not only traditions *within* the religion but also between their church traditions and other social, cultural, and political ideologies they likewise embrace *as traditions*.

Years of observation and reflection have led me to recognize in Catholics' often passionate insistences upon something as traditional the unspoken assumption that the words or symbols or roles are *naturally* so, having been so from time immemorial. Not just a matter of, "This is the way it's always done, the traditional way" (note the indefinite, passive voice), there is often a sense of something powerful at stake in situations of differing expectations or disagreements, implicit in the insistence, "It *has* to be this way (otherwise, what will people *think*?)." I can attest as both a Catholic priest and, earlier in young adulthood, a church organist that many in both guilds can be heard to opine, "I'll take a dozen funerals over one wedding any day!" That lament testifies to the extent to which the lay agents of the marriage rites, typically the brides and their mothers but by no means to the exclusion (increasingly) of the principal male agents, exercise robustly

6. Bell, *Ritual Theory*, 192–93.

(often aggressively) their own power in negotiating the ideology of Christian marriage through their particular ritualizing thereof.

The following narrative plots an itinerary of sorts, whereby my practical work as a professor and pastoral minister has brought home for me just how great indeed are the degrees of ideological negotiation entailed in the practice of the marriage rite (and thus, the "institution" of marriage) in white, middle-class sectors of US Catholicism. I begin from my experience in the undergraduate core-theology classroom, a venue felicitous to my rehearsing something of the current Roman Catholic theology (meaning) of marriage within a sacramental anthropology and ecclesiology that, nonetheless, inevitably encounters contestation (challenges, disagreements) in ritual practice.

The Sacramentality of Marriage: Agreement in Principle, Contestation in Ritual

During my fifteen-year tenure on the faculty of a large national Catholic university, I regularly taught a section of the theology department's year-long core course, "Exploring Catholicism: Tradition and Transition," to a class of approximately forty undergraduates. The mandate for the second semester was for ecclesiology, sacramental theology, and spirituality. I rearranged the order and took some liberty of interpretation, such that I began with sacramental-liturgical theology, moved on to ecclesiology, and concluded with moral theology, as I remained convinced college-age students are more interested in ethical issues and case studies than discussions of lofty, often abstract spiritualities. That practical angle[7] was paramount in my approach from the semester's start with sacraments, for which I had the students read in tandem a work in systematic theology, Bernard Cooke's *Sacraments & Sacramentality*, and a thematically edited collection in practical-liturgical theology, *Bodies of Worship: Explorations in Theory and Practice*.

To follow Cooke's original (indeed, controversial) appropriation of Rahner and Schillebeeckx in his phenomenology of symbol and communication, personhood and community, is to arrive at marriage (not baptism or Eucharist) as the starting point for discussing the seven official sacraments in the Roman Catholic Church. Cooke's text meets still-adolescent college

---

7. For a description of my methodology for that course see, Morrill, "Liturgical Theology," 9–12.

students where they are; namely, in the process of discovering their senses of identity through a growing capacity to think reflexively, the realization that all experience is interpreted experience, and a comprehension of how that interpretation takes place only through symbolizing (for which word is fundamental). Sacrament is the term for any symbol or symbolic process revelatory of the (totally other) God beyond our sensing who, biblical tradition attests, communes with humanity personally, that is, through the limited but powerful reality of inter-subjective and communal life. Cooke arrives at this summary statement:

> If we restrict "sacrament" to certain liturgical rituals, it is logical to think of baptism as the initial sacrament. If, however, we realize the fundamental sacramentality of all human experience and the way Jesus transformed this sacramentality, there is good reason for seeing human friendship as the most basic sacrament of God's saving presence among us. Human friendship reflects and makes credible the reality of God's love for humans. . . . Within human friendship there is a paradigmatic role played by the love between a Christian wife and husband. Building on the transformation of marriage's meaning that began with the Israelitic prophets, Christianity sees the love relationship of a Christian couple as sacramentalizing the relationship between Christ and the church, between God and humankind. God's saving action consists essentially in the divine self-giving [grace]. This is expressed by and present in the couple's self-gift to each other; they are sacrament to each other, to their children, and to their fellow Christians. This sacramentality, though specifically instanced in Christian marriage, extends to all genuine human friendship.[8]

Cooke's theology creatively builds on the official theology of the Church, as presented in the Introduction to the Rite of Marriage, which reiterates the Second Vatican Council's bold advance in asserting that the couple are, together and to each other, God's offer of salvation and working out of their sanctification, and in that a living, personal sign of God's love to the world.[9]

---

8. Cooke, *Sacraments*, 91. Cooke himself came to address explicitly the power dimensions of symbol (word and image) and ritual, among some dozen forms of human power as these intersect with the divine ways revealed in Scripture, in his *Power and the Spirit of God*, 121–55. For a Protestant treatment of human friendship as revelatory of divine presence, the activity of the Spirit of God, see the penultimate chapter in Moltmann, *Spirit of Life*.

9. See "Rite of Marriage," nos. 1–4; see also "Order of Matrimony," nos. 1–2, 8. See also Paul VI, *Lumen Gentium*, no. 11. The fullest elaboration comes in the Vatican Council's

The post-Vatican II Rite of Marriage itself, in its various ritual elements, serves to bring this about, that is, to actualize this union through the virtual space the ritual creates for the couple to reshape their identities in relation to each other.

To speak of virtual space is to profit from Bruce Kapferer's original contribution for theorizing about the "inner dynamics of rite as the potency of the capacity of ritual to alter, change, or transform the existential circumstances of persons."[10] Ritualizing enables people explicitly to negotiate what the "chaotic" character of the quotidian, non-ritual "lived world" is incapable of engaging:

> [The] virtuality of ritual reality is really real, a complete and filled-out existential reality—but in its own terms. . . . By entering within the particular dynamics of life by means of the virtuality of ritual, ritualists engage with positioning and structurating processes that are otherwise impossible to address in the tempo and dynamics of ordinary lived processes as these are lived on the surface.[11]

Precisely on that terrain of ritual agency is where, I discovered, contestation arises for young American Catholics as they imagine and celebrate the Rite of Marriage.

I found my students receptive if not enthused about Cooke's theology in all its concreteness and incarnational honoring of human agency and identity as exercised in friendship, broadly conceived, and marriage, specifically examined. Turning from the systematic theology of meaning to the liturgical theology of ritual, on the other hand, was another matter. For that I availed myself of marriage-rite specialist Paul Covino's chapter in *Bodies of Worship* and his thirty-minute video, *Our Catholic Wedding*.[12] In both text and video, Covino's approach to the Catholic wedding ritual relentlessly advocates practices based on what he distills as the fundamentals in the theology (meaning) of the sacrament; namely, (1) the couple as agents of their personal union and, thus, as sacraments of the church, itself being

---

final document: "Authentic married love is caught up into divine love and is governed and enriched by Christ's redeeming power and the saving activity of the Church, so that this love may lead the spouses to God with powerful effect and may aid and strengthen them in the sublime office of being a father or a mother." Paul VI, *Gaudium et Spes*, no. 48.

10. Kapferer, "Ritual Dynamics," 47.

11. Kapferer, "Ritual Dynamics," 47–48.

12. See Covino, "Christian Marriage," 107–19; and Covino and Fleming, *Our Catholic Wedding*.

the "sacrament of unity," the people as one in Christ, and (2) the "corporate dimension" of the marriage rite by its very nature *as liturgy*, citing "Vatican II's strong preference for 'communal celebration involving the presence and active participation of the faithful . . . to a celebration that is individual and quasi-private."[13] Covino rues the extent to which US Catholic couples remain "uninterested in or even resistant to promoting communal participation in the wedding liturgy," thereby causing "Catholics who actively participate in Sunday Mass [to] succumb to the social custom of attending weddings as polite, but passive, observers."[14] Both book chapter and video (comprised of footage from the actual, real-time wedding of a young couple, interspersed with "talking head" comments by the bride, groom, their parents, and Pastor Fleming) entail Covino's commentary on the major steps of the ritual, from entrance procession forward, arguing for how (and *why*) he has shaped each element of the rite over the years: "Together, these practices have helped to overcome the cultural tendency toward passivity at weddings, and create an assembly that is ready to celebrate the wedding liturgy as a corporate body" and "a better enfleshment of the Catholic faith concerning marriage."[15]

Ah, but therein lies the rub! Is not Covino's assumption that a prior set of meanings (a totalistic, static ideology) of the marital sacrament somehow exists and needs only be ritually expressed? To my viewing of the video, the bride and groom and parents do not seem to articulate anything specific about the official Church theology of marriage or its rite; rather, their comments basically run along the lines of vague feelings of togetherness, welcome, and inclusivity of guests. But, my perceptions aside, what interested (and continues to interest) me the most were the students' responses to the video. Every year, as I entered the three-session marriage unit of my Catholicism core course, I began by showing the video and then opening the floor for discussion with, "So, what'd you think?" One year, a particularly bright, engaged, articulate, un-self-conscious young woman seated in the back of the large classroom (the type of student an undergrad professor prays for), instantly blurted out, "That ruined everything I've dreamed for my wedding since I was four years old!" ("Yippee, let's go!" I thought gleefully to myself.) "How so?" I replied professorially to her.

13. Covino, "Christian Marriage," 109. Internal citation from Paul VI, *Sacrosanctum Concilium*, no. 27.

14. Covino, "Christian Marriage," 109.

15. Covino, "Christian Marriage," 111, 113.

My student was readily able to list key features of the ritual, as she had been imagining them since preschool. I list them here in contrast to what Covino advocates as the logical ritual expressions of the reformed Catholic theology of marriage: the bride hidden from sight until the guests turn dramatically toward the back of the church for her dazzling epiphany at the foot of the aisle (versus the couple and both sets of parents standing in the doorway to greet the guests as they arrive for the ceremony); the bride on her proud, adoring father's arm, appearing only after a sufficient pause, and even change to heraldic music following the procession of single bridesmaids, and, even prior to that, the singular seating of the bride's mother (versus the Rite of Marriage's description of the procession as including, all together, the ministers [acolytes and lectors], priest, bride, and groom and, optionally, "at least their parents and the two witnesses"[16]); the guests positioned in couples or single family units along opposite edges of the pews—"Bride or groom?" ushers ask when seating guests—all the way down the aisle, while professionally performed music wafts overhead (versus groomsmen and bridesmaids seating everybody anywhere and across entire pews, so as "to encourage people to form a cohesive assembly," while a cantor rehearses all in the ritual music prior to the start of the service[17]); bride and groom, flanked by the maid of honor and best man, positioned from the start at the top step of the sanctuary, backs to the people, the maid of honor having arranged the substantial train of the bridal gown to flow down the steps (versus the couple themselves sitting in the front row of the assembly or at one side of the sanctuary, only to step to the center-front of the sanctuary at the end of the Liturgy of the Word for the exchange of consent and rings); bride and groom quietly repeating their vows after the priest, who faces them in the sanctuary, their backs to the people (versus the priest moving to the head of the aisle, between the front row of pews, while bride and groom stand front and center in the sanctuary, facing out to the assembly). In addition, Covino encourages the couple's ministering cups of the eucharistic wine (the blood of Christ) to the assembly during the Communion Rite[18] (versus their typically kneeling close to the altar table, backs to the assembly, or in many cases, being seated to revel

16. "Rite of Marriage," no. 20.

17. Covino, "Christian Marriage," 112.

18. Covino's recommendation here is of a sort the Vatican subsequently prohibited, unless bride and/or groom are duly instituted extraordinary ministers of Holy Communion. See Congregation for Divine Worship, *Redemptionis Sacramentum*, nos. 154–60.

reflectively or quietly smile or even gesture at their guests as they reach the front of the Communion line).

Repulsed by Covino's practical interpretive implementation of the ritual details and overall theology of the reformed Roman Catholic Rite of Marriage, my twenty-year-old college student's priorities exuded the popular and commercial cultures' criteria for a "fairy-tale wedding." Indeed, that was the very title the press used for the royal nuptials of Will and Kate and, again, in the news and entertainment media's obligatory year-in-review exercises during the last days of 2011. My point here is not to deride the multi-million-dollar bridal industry or decades-long (often centuries-long) Euro-American wedding ceremonial customs and superstitions. I wish, rather, to articulate their evident function as fundamental sources for Americans' (Catholics as much as others)—especially brides and their mothers'—vehemently held convictions for what constitutes a suitable if not powerfully impressive wedding. Perhaps most notable is the fact that the bride-to-be, as early as age four, has a strong sense of her agency (power) in shaping and controlling all aspects of the ritual, with her mother expected and expecting to hold the key supporting role as critical advisor, sometimes in conflict with the bride but always allied with the bride as her advocate toward their hired service providers—photographer, florist, caterer, musicians for church and reception, *and* the officiating minister. The wedding, *pace* Covino's passionate convictions and efforts, is a private family affair and, as such, ritually actualizes the basic way in which the vast majority of late-modern US Catholics practice (and *thereby* understand) their marriages as private, interpersonal commitments (expecting ongoing support from family and friends) between the couple. My impression from both classroom teaching and pastoral work with wedding couples is that they do indeed sense what Cooke theologizes as sacramentality in the marriage relationship, but with one key difference. Their practical theologies of Christian marriage lack a strong ecclesial dimension, or at least an ecclesiology in which institution, including authoritative teaching and officials as well as public (Covino's "corporate") ritual, figures integrally.

Moving from the shaping of their wedding ceremonies forward into marital domesticity, the overwhelming majority of lay Catholics reject the Roman hierarchy's repeated insistences that the use of contraceptives even in marriage is grave matter for mortal sin.[19] Contraception and child

19. Year after year, in teaching my concluding unit on moral theology in that core Catholicism course, taking the students through a close, historical-theologically informed

rearing, they counter, is a private matter for the couple, to be worked out personally on the basis of a wide range of criteria—social, economic, and religious. Indeed, many American Catholic couples (not unlike British Anglicans Prince William and Kate Middleton) cohabitate for extended periods prior to formal marriage. This fact has, I must confess, at times sparked my incredulity over the manner and extent to which I have found couples clinging to superstitions and medieval-era symbolic conventions in the execution of their wedding ceremonies. For the last part of this essay, then, I shall turn to one detail in practice that arrested my attention when presiding over a wedding and opens the way to considering further how likely it most often is the case that people's ideologies of marriage are, as Clifford Geertz said of religion generally, not so much "well-formulated beliefs" as "collections of notions."[20]

Ideology as Ritual Activity:
Practical Executions of the Marriage Rite

This is not to imply that the notions, however disjointed compared to the normative liturgical ordo and formal theology of marriage, do not in their cumulative execution provide the ritual-actors a feeling of well-being. No, it is just that this well-being rests not on well-formulated beliefs but, rather, in the (inchoate) promise arising from *well-doing*, that is, from the adequate if not elegant execution of the several gestures, words, and poses that are "right" or "natural" to a good and proper (traditional) wedding. This affective rightness or naturalness that the performers of the rite—bride, groom, mothers, and attendants—feel at various points and overall in the ceremony (and thereafter upon reflection) is what Bell is driving at in arguing for ritual as a strategic mode of practice wherein people negotiate their power and positions (their performative identities) within a social as well as, most often, a cosmic order.

Take, for example, the custom prohibiting the groom from seeing the bride on the day of the wedding prior to the opening of the ceremony, lest they bring "bad luck" down upon themselves. A performative element utterly outside the ritual frame and ideology of the current Roman Catholic

---

reading of Pope John Paul II's 1995 encyclical *Evangelium Vitae*, I found the students dumbfounded to learn of the church's official condemnation of artificial contraception within marriage. That proved to be complete news to nearly all those cradle Catholics.

20. See Bell, *Ritual Theory*, 184–85.

Rite of Marriage, this superstition would also seem beyond the pale for university-educated middle-class Americans. And yet, I recall how in preparing two affluent professionals in their late-twenties for their wedding, I had proposed that they together greet their guests as they arrived at the church and then process into the ceremony, each on the arms of their respective parents. Surprised yet attracted by the suggestion, they seemed to adopt it warmly. Yet on the day of the celebration, I found the groom in the entry of the church, along with the rest of the attending party, but not the bride. He explained that the couple subsequently agreed that his seeing her in her bridal dress prior to her processing down the aisle would be bad luck. I simply smiled and shrugged it off, for, after all, their happiness and peace of mind was of paramount importance.

Still, I could not help musing, both then and now years later, at how the couple renegotiated that strategy on their own—that is, apart from the priest with whom they had made the preparations—but, moreover, at how vitally important that ritual-symbolic detail was to the two of them. The conclusion I have come to draw from this small example (which nonetheless was a truly big deal to that groom and bride) is that the archaic practice of hiding the bride from the groom, as part of the long-abandoned ideology of European arranged marriages transferring possession of a woman (and her dowry) from one man to another, has in all its strangeness retained its force in conveying how much is at stake in what is about to take place in the wedding ceremony. As Kapferer and Handelman have each argued in their own ways, it is precisely the very oddity or strangeness of many rituals in their actual contexts—their non-representational or directly causative significance—that enables them to draw their performers into a deep, self-enclosed "phenomenal pocket"[21] or "virtual space"[22] wherein the ritual-actors may realize for themselves (bodily, semiotically) something of their own singular, interpersonal, or social agency at which they could not arrive by argument or explanation. At my present theoretical ("expert") distance, I would argue that for this couple, who had been cohabitating for several years, their careful avoidance of physically even laying eyes on each other the day of their wedding was a performance of how deeply and how much they sensed was at stake in what they were about to do with and for their relationship, how deeply they desired that their love and partnership not suffer misfortune but, on the contrary, endure and even thrive, how

21. See Handelman, "Introduction," 10–17.
22. See Kapferer, "Ritual Dynamics," 46–48.

poignantly they knew of both the positive and negative forces—natural and supernatural—their world portended for their marriage. In this one can, to follow Bell's lead, recognize the couple ritually enacting their own ideology of marriage in a highly complex social (economic, class, religious, national, ethnic, and pluralistic) context.

Were space to allow for a more extensive treatment of my experiences of the Rite of Marriage in actual practice, I would similarly discuss in detail such dichotomies between the official ritual text, along with expert guidelines for performance, and the conventional middle-class-American expectations for practice as I listed from my earlier classroom account. Here I must simply attest that I have come to find in my practical, pastoral experiences of presiding at US Catholic weddings strong evidence to support Kapferer's insightful theory of "ritual as a virtuality," wherein he seeks "to push ritual as a radical suspension of ordinary realities" in such a direction as

> to suggest that it is the very disjunction of the world of rite from its larger context that contributes to the force of much ritual dynamics. I add to this notion the nonrepresentational character of the world of rite as this is formed in its disjunctive space. I mean by this that the processes of rites are not always to be conceived of as directly reflective of outer realities, as has been the thrust of conventional symbolic analyses. This is not to say that they do not grasp or represent meanings that are integral to broad, abstract cosmological notions. . . . They may even be metaphoric of larger processes, but this is secondary, frequently an analytic construction made by scholars who maintain themselves as being external to the phenomenon in question and committed to other rationalities.[23]

The very weirdness of many customary practices is often what makes the virtual space of ritual so existentially transformative for the agential identities of its performers. This theoretical insight goes a long way in helping explain why, for example, brides (as well as, at times, their grooms) hold to a processional choreography that a ritual critic might perceive as bespeaking patriarchy (that is, a father's delivery of a bride, veiled, complete with dowry).

23. Kapferer, "Ritual Dynamics," 46.

By contrast, Covino, in his analytic distancing from the popular bridal culture, exemplifies the bias of the (external) expert when he argues the following:

> Most women today would resent the implication that they are being "given away" by one man to another, yet there is still strong emotional attachment to this form of the wedding entrance procession. "Tradition," a wise person once said, "is the living faith of the dead. Traditionalism is the dead faith of the living." The customary American form of the wedding entrance procession seems no longer to reflect what we actually believe about marriage, as Americans and as Catholics. It would be safe to say that this is a case of traditionalism, not tradition.[24]

Rather, I would proffer, it would be safe to say that Covino's essay proves to be a case of what Kapferer, along with Bell in her own way, have identified as the ideological-theoretical blinders the ritual theorist can unknowingly wear. Here, Covino is stumped in trying to explain why American Catholics persist in this type of processional practice because his (modern) insistence on a totalizing concept for the entire marriage rite fails to recognize that a given bride's notions of *her* Catholic Church ceremony most likely include the ideal of the "fairy-tale wedding"—a virtual ritual space that is really real, and all the more virtual, given its mediation through digital technology: the magazines, websites, movie scenes, and marketing that altogether shape the "picture-perfect wedding." That plethora of influences upon the bride and groom's imagining of the virtual space of their wedding certainly puts pressure on their ritual agency, but still most often especially on that of the bride, who senses that other women will judge her accountable for whether the "wedding went off well."[25]

The Rite of Marriage Going Forward: Indications of Creativity and Crisis

Still, middle-aged folk (such as myself) would be mistaken in thinking that contemporary American brides and wedding couples largely experience

---

24. Covino, "Christian Marriage," 114.

25. I am indebted to members of the Emerging Critical Resources for Liturgical Studies seminar of the North American Academy of Liturgy, who provided me with this and other insights while discussing my first draft of this essay during a session at the annual meeting in Montreal, January 6, 2012.

themselves as totally constricted by media culture, fairy-tale ideals, marketing campaigns and, yes, ecclesial ritual books and clerical authorities. Not only is the construction of one's "perfect" wedding a creative project for which great numbers of brides take charge, but also couples increasingly expect to be able to negotiate together their own decisions about how to put the religious ceremony together and, indeed, whether to have such a ceremony as part of their wedding at all. One final anecdote can serve as an indicator of the still significantly changing ideologies young American Catholics are practicing as they approach and execute the Rite of Marriage.

Several years ago, I presided over the wedding of a former student who, along with his bride, had majored in theology at the Catholic university where I had been teaching. As we three went through the official text several months in advance, the couple embraced a number of elements of the rite distinctive from the conventional "fairy-tale" or industry-driven imagery, including an order of procession that included not only the ministers but also the groom with his parents, followed by the bride with hers; the couple's standing at the center of sanctuary facing out to the assembly for the act of consent (exchange of vows), and the couple's serving the assembly as ministers of the cup during the Communion Rite. During the rehearsal, however, on the eve of the wedding day and with many people in attendance, the three of us came upon a ritual impasse.

Well into the course of the rehearsal, as I positioned them front and center in the sanctuary for the act of consent (exchange of vows and rings), the groom informed me that he and the bride had written their own vows. I was floored by this and had to reply straightforwardly that what they wanted to do was impossible for me to carry out. I explained that Roman Catholic canon and liturgical law together prescribe what constitutes the proper matter and form for a valid performance of a sacrament. In the case of marriage, the matter is comprised of the couple themselves, freely entering into the marital covenant, while the form is their speaking to each the words of consent in the official ritual text (for which in the US dioceses there are two options). Their pronouncing other words would not constitute their having validly celebrated the sacramental Rite of Marriage. My explanation, I could perceive, was lost on the couple, with the groom telling me he had never heard of such rules and could not see why I was imposing them. I told him I could not negotiate this point, but what I could suggest would be for them to share their words with each other and for the assembly in the concluding rite of the service, that is, after the meditation and prayer after Communion. Unhappy but also able to see that such was my "final offer," the couple agreed to the compromise.

That pastoral-liturgical incident is indicative of a distinctive feature of the late-modern milieu of American weddings; namely, an assertion of the uniqueness of the couple involved that demands explicit, original expression in formal traditional and religious ritual itself. This is not to deny that traditions, including ritual traditions, always entail change; however, the degree to which the laity consciously pursue individual creativity and explicitly demand of the officials innovations in the ritual forms constitutes a new wrinkle in the overlapping folds of this and other rituals' histories of practice. In the case of Euro-American Catholicism (such is the stated limit of my study here), the marriage rate among the younger generations has been decreasing steadily, reflecting that within the wider population. While multiple social forces are contributing to this phenomenon, one factor surely is the dissonance many Catholic laity experience between their human agency and religious ideology and the ideology of the official, expert class of their church; namely, the bishops and clergy. The overall situation would seem to be an instance of what Bell argues can take place when leaders "on higher levels of social organization" (in this case, the clerical hierarchy of the church) ritually construct power in relation to "the micro-relations of power that shape daily life on the lower levels of the society" (namely, the laity in the church): "changes in the latter level can precipitate a crisis in which the demands of ritual to conform to traditional models clash with the ability of those rites to resonate with the real experiences of the social body."[26]

That last pastoral-liturgical scenario I recounted indicates the degree to which US Catholic couples increasingly expect to be able to take creative license, as it were, with the official Rite of Marriage, but a further alienation between hierarchy and laity seems to be accelerating as well; namely, the decision of couples to forego the sacramental rite entirely. For some, this is a matter of their ideologies of marriage or even the religion in general being at odds with the official teachings, regulations, and ritual procedures of the church, such that they would not even consider a "Catholic church wedding." For others, however, the alienation is not so comprehensive but, rather, against the specific practices and procedures the hierarchy requires for preparing and executing the Rite of Marriage, such as the restriction of the celebration to consecrated church spaces (e.g., churches, chapels,

26. Bell, *Ritual Theory*, 213.

oratories), a specified amount of marital preparation through either classes or a retreat program, or the prohibition of substituting secular literature or sacred texts from other religious or cultural traditions for biblical readings in the marriage celebration's Liturgy of the Word. Across the range of alternate practices, one cannot help but perceive the performances of real breaks (crises) between the official ideology of marriage for the Church and the Christian agential identity many younger Catholics are forging as they construct their own ideologies of marriage with partners variably of their own or other or no religious traditions and, with the change in civil marital law, even with (same-sex) partners the official Church explicitly prohibits.

3

Eucharist

Ritual and Moral Agency in Holy Communion

Introduction

DURING THE 1990S, THE discipline of liturgical theology in North America witnessed multiple constructive attempts at articulating the intrinsic relationship between the church's ritual celebration of worship and the irreducible ethical dimension of the life of faith the gospel demands. The efforts spanned the ecumenical spectrum, with notable book-length treatments by Methodist Don Saliers and Roman Catholic Kevin Irwin appearing in the same year (1994) and offering similar arguments for the necessity of adding to the patristic adage, *lex orandi, lex credendi,* a third element, *lex vivendi*[1] (or *agendi*[2]), so as to clarify that the "law of belief" established by the "law of prayer" is not a matter of merely asserting doctrinal concepts but, rather, an agenda for living. The first two volumes of Lutheran Gordon Lathrop's trilogy[3] framed the moment, while my own attempt at integrating political and liturgical theology through the ethical-memorial character of the Eucharist[4] reached publication at decade's end. Common to all four of

1. See Saliers, *Worship*, 185–88.
2. See Irwin, *Context*, 311–46.
3. See Lathrop, *Holy Things*, 204–25; and Lathrop, *Holy People*.
4. See Morrill, *Anamnesis*, 139–88.

us authors was the influence of the Russian Orthodox Alexander Schmemann, whose tight little corpus of passionate prose pressed for a recovery
of Christian liturgy's primordial purpose as revealing an entire vision of
life, as his still widely read book puts it, *For the Life of the World*.[5] Schmemann traveled the globe tirelessly until his early death to cancer in 1983,
answering invitations to speak not only to Orthodox audiences, but to a
great variety of ecclesial bodies on the content and form of the liturgy as the
key to embracing life in this world as God's project, the kingdom of God.
And yet, he repeatedly bemoaned how the import of his message missed
the mark of his largely enchanted listeners (and readers).[6] While writing
my doctoral dissertation and in the first years of my professional career
thereafter I found my lectures—so deeply inspired by Schmemann and his
ecumenical followers—often falling upon a similar fate. I would like to recount one such tale at the outset here so as to introduce the basic problem
and its corollaries that comprise my present wrestling with the relationship
between liturgy and ethics.

Liturgy and Ethics: Sweeping Theory versus
Practical, Particular Questions

A few years after completing my PhD at Emory University and taking my
faculty position at Boston College, I received an invitation from Holy Spirit
Catholic Church back in Atlanta to fly down and give a talk for their Sunday
morning adult education series, a long running, strongly attended program
impressive for an American Catholic parish. The deacon who contacted
me said they would like me to discuss the Eucharist and I, in turn, asked
if they had any particular aspects of the Mass in mind. Receiving the reply
that no, the approach was up to me, I decided to exploit the name of their
parish, entitling the talk: "Liturgy of the Church: Work of the People, Work
of the Spirit." The lecture would unpack the Vatican II recovery of the concept of liturgy as a participatory action of the assembled church, as well as
the promise—pastoral, ethically formative, ecclesial, and ecumenical—of
recognizing the agency of the Holy Spirit in the roles and actions of all assembled, as opposed to the (apostolically successive) clergy imaging Christ
to the observant laity. Such would, in my estimation, amount to a lecture

5. See Schmemann, *For the Life*, 37–39, 44–46, 139–40, 147–50.

6. See, for example, Schmemann, *Eucharist*, 144–46; and Schmemann, *Journals*,
122–24. See also Morrill, *Anamnesis*, 84–87; and Morrill, "Liturgical Is Political," 52–54.

that would expand the knowledge and stretch the imaginations of these parishioners—something both interesting and challenging for them. I wanted (1) to press the traditional roots of the revised Mass of Paul VI, (2) to demonstrate the work of the Spirit in proclaimed Word and shared sacrament as shaping the practical lives of faithful participants, and (3) to expound on the ecumenical character of such a pneumatological understanding and practice of the liturgy. Such were the goals and contours of my Sunday morning lecture, the content and style of which were in the encompassing theological genre of Schmemann and others whose liturgical theologies I had found so inspiring. Here is a one-paragraph summary of the ethically formative vision I elicited from rejuvenated liturgical tradition:

The key to the ongoing reform and renewal of the Church's liturgy lies in practicing it as a privileged, indeed singular, form of knowing and experiencing the freedom of the gospel. Christians today must come to the table of God's Word and the Eucharist[7] not to confirm uncritically the ways in which our society tends to measure our importance and self-worth (such as incomes, houses, automobiles), but to open ourselves over and again to the Spirit of Christ who reveals through Scripture and sacramental tradition how we are Christ's body now in the world. The sacrament of confirmation makes us *subjects* of the eucharistic action, changing us from passive observers of a religious ritual into active participants receiving anew, during every eucharistic prayer, the power of the Holy Spirit invoked both on the bread and wine *and upon those who have assembled to share it.* If the sacramental rites of the Church make use of a wide array of sacred objects, symbolic gestures, and ritual personages, this is not to make those who have assembled passive observers of a religious spectacle but, rather, to reveal to them the divine glory that is hidden in every human body and shared among all people of good will (see Luke 2:14). This evangelical-ethical approach to liturgy is a challenge for all in the Church today, but one worthy of the baptism in which all have been immortalized for lives of Christ-like service, in love with the world that he came to save and will one day return to gather into a new heavens and a new earth (see Rev 21:1; 2 Pet 3:13).

Ta da! The hundred people comprising my Sunday morning audience gave me a nice round of applause, after which I invited questions. First off the mark: "Father, why can't my wife, who is Methodist, receive Communion with me when she comes to Mass? And why am I not supposed to take

7. See Paul VI, *Dei Verbum*, no. 21.

Communion when I go to her church?" Many heads immediately nodded, people turning briefly to each other in enthusiastic anticipation of my reply. It was a question-cum-statement that truly gave me pause. The people had patiently listened to my sweeping, fervent vision of liturgy and life as world-transforming mission, it seemed, so as finally to get to ask the theologian what really mattered to them: the Roman regulations restricting access to Holy Communion. These middle-to-upper-class New South Catholics, so regular in Mass attendance and supportive of their pastor and extensive parish staff, had highly practical, pastoral—really, critical—concerns about the relationship between liturgy and life that I had simply not anticipated. I had sought to inspire the folks with an appreciative knowledge of the elements of the rite that could open into new awareness for participation, but what was on many of their minds was the boundary cutting off such participation with and for the very people with whom they sacramentally share their Christian vocations; namely, their wives and husbands.[8]

I decided that the first thing needed in reply was a presentation about the facts of Roman Catholic Church polity (canon and liturgical law), so that all in the room might be aware of the official ecclesial parameters of the problem. But I suspect that to my audience, that sounded like the massive shift in methodology from my biblically, patristically, ecumenically inspired talk that it was. The questions kept coming, pressing me to explain the history of schisms and the Roman Catholic doctrine of apostolic succession and the necessity of union with the bishop of Rome. I suspect many in the room already knew some or all of that, while others did not, but I could also sense that I was struggling to get at the heart of what these practicing Catholics experienced as the fundamental question about liturgy and ethics: The dignity of every person—perhaps, even more pointedly, of all the baptized—goes on the line in the Communion procession. As I have continued to reflect on the discussion I shared with the Holy Spirit parishioners, I have been trying to conceive how liturgical theology (second-order theology) can adequately take account of, indeed, may need to give priority to, the contexts of celebration in theorizing about liturgical practice as formative of Christian ethical agents. Ecclesiology—a highly practical, historically situated ecclesiology oriented to the ritual body—must be addressed when arguing (with the use of traditional and historical *texts*) for what the Spirit of the crucified and risen Christ offers believers through

8. See Paul VI, *Lumen Gentium*, nos. 35, 41; and Paul VI, *Gaudium et Spes*, nos. 48–50.

liturgical participation in the paschal mystery. Attention to the particular elements of rite that actually grasp the imagination of the faithful might be a good starting place.

Over the past decade the Communion procession, access to Holy Communion has emerged as a key test case for popular theologizing about liturgy and ethics in the American Catholic Church. Functioning on interpersonal and local levels as a problem for "mixed marriages," the ecclesial-ethical dilemma of eucharistic participation has taken on a wider societal character in the electoral cycles of the American political system. I am referring here, of course, to the strategy of various US Catholic bishops to declare publicly that specific candidates for governmental office are banned from receiving Holy Communion in their dioceses. The reason for the prohibition is the inconsistency of the candidate's legislative record and campaign platform with the church's official teaching concerning abortion. As public figures, those politicians embody—that is, they function as personae—of the principles, values, and affections of not only the American nation but also, at least in the eyes of the Catholic hierarchy and some laity, the Church as well. Scandal, a serious threat to the health of the social body of the church, those bishops are effectively arguing, is at issue, and thus cannot be ignored. In many cases, the bishops also declare their pastoral responsibility to call to repentance the politician, whose eternal soul is in danger. Still, many (often even the majority of) American Catholics, as scientific polling data of election results indicate, do not judge these Catholic politicians in the same way. Indeed, their criteria for what constitutes scandal are quite different. Imbued with varying degrees of what social theorists describe as communitarianism and liberalism, many protest—some in print, far more in conversation—that the bishops are politicizing the public office holder's faith, which is properly a personal matter.

Stepping back here, in the forum of an academic essay, I would argue that this question of ecclesial discipline and sacramental polity is rightly political—a politicized issue—because the liturgy of the Church itself is a type of political act. Here I shall draw upon the work of Bernd Wannenwetsch, a German Lutheran ethicist, to elucidate something of the political dimension of Christian worship before turning to historical and anthropological evidence for the Communion procession as a particularly powerful element of the Eucharist, because constitutive, in part, of the moral agency of the members of the Church.

Liturgical Worship as Political Practice, as Ethical Socialization

Setting aside conventional modern notions of politics, Wannenwetsch argues that the Church's liturgical worship is "inescapably political," for in assembling to engage in word and sacrament, its members are "transposed into a social order . . . aligned towards the recognition of the good that comes from God, towards the common exploration of the good in the world, and towards the trying and testing of that good in shared action."[9] Worship is a non-foundational ethical source for the lives of the faithful, for it is participation in liturgy itself that forms their perceptions, imaginations, and judgments according to the ethos of the revelation of God. The inherent conceptual dimension of the ethos of God's judgment and actions experienced in the liturgy theological ethics reflects upon the inherent conceptual dimension of the ethos of God's judgment and actions experienced in the liturgy, bringing that ethos to bear upon the issues and decisions the faithful engage in their daily lives in the larger world. But it is, nonetheless, in the enactment of the assembly itself, the *communio* they share,[10] that the members of the church "find a specific, social form of life" that is "their basic *political existence.*"[11]

While scholarly and popular Christian ethics enlist multiple sources for reflection and judgment (Scripture, history, philosophies, etc.), the liturgy plays a uniquely important function due to its own way of bringing the canon of Scripture (which Wannenwetsch acutely notes "was established precisely for the requirements of worship") and others of those same sources together to construct "a comprehensive sensory, intellectual, and spiritual experience. This is worship as a form of life."[12] No autonomous exercise of reason at one's desk, worship is socially dramatic as it continuously wrestles with the "pathos and ethos" of life:

> [W]e must remember that worship is not a linear, harmonious socialization process, in which the ethical shaping of believers follows like words written one after another on a blank page. Ethical learning always proceeds in the form of a struggle between the "old" and the "new" man. As Paul says in his famous paraclesis

9. Wannenwetsch, *Political Worship*, 9.

10. Wannenwetsch employs but does not elaborate on this crucial concept. For constructive treatments and bibliographies, see Cooke, "Body," 39–50; and Cooke, *Distancing,* 287.

11 Wannenwetsch, *Political Worship*, 7.

12. Wannenwetsch, *Political Worship*, 14.

at the beginning of Romans 12, it is a matter of the new *morphe* of the Christian life. . . . Although "the form of this world" is destined to pass away (1 Cor. 7:31), he evidently, for all that, assigns it to the effective formative powers which put an almost irresistible spell on human beings. Even Christians are not always free of their influence; they need the reminder (the "consoling admonition": *paraklesis*) of their freedom in Christ. These "proofs of God's mercy" (*oiktirmoi*, Rom 12:1), which Paul has talked about in the previous chapters, must be continually kept before eyes and ears. So the transformation required is expected and promoted not by an iron will but emphatically through the "renewal of your mind," the *nous* as the organ of perception in the widest sense—practical judgement.[13]

Whereas Wannenwetsch draws primarily on Paul's Letter to the Romans here, liturgical theologians (myself included) have most often turned to First Corinthians 11, Paul's admonition of their eucharistic assemblies, as a primordial source for the Eucharist's meaning and purpose. Allow me to revisit that Pauline text yet again, for it surely anchors eucharistic tradition as intrinsically social and ethically oriented.[14]

What we find in 1 Corinthians 11 is not only one of the earliest definitions of tradition in the Church but also one of the first teachings about the Eucharist. Paul is able to *hand on* (v. 23) to the Corinthians the origin of the Church's eucharistic meal in Jesus' words and gestures at the supper on the eve of his death. His passing on of the tradition is occasioned, nonetheless, by unacceptable reports about their assemblies. Paul perceives the conventional social behavior of the wealthier Christians as defeating the very action of communion in the body and blood of Christ that they should be enacting. Paul instructs the wealthier members to recognize what they are doing when they feast together while the poorer members, lacking the time and money to join, feel humiliated. Such selfish feasting unmasks a character inimical to that of Christ, whom the community claims to commemorate in the performance of the Lord's Supper. The failure to discern the body of the Lord that brings condemnatory judgment upon them (v. 28) is not, as has so long been the anachronistic interpretation by Roman

13. Wannenwetsch, *Political Worship*, 37. The affinity of Wannenwetsch's thought and philosophical resources (including Wittgenstein) with that of Don Saliers (whom he nowhere cites) is most evident in this conceptualization of pathos and ethos in liturgy. See Saliers, *Worship*, 21–38.

14. For discussion of the passage with reference to the works of Xavier Léon-Dufour and Jerome Murphy-O'Connor, see Morrill, "Struggle," 68–71.

Catholics, a matter of recognizing the real presence of Christ in the bread and wine, but rather of abandoning their society's standards so as to conform their lives to Christ's. Faithfulness to eucharistic tradition requires a discernment of Christ's body in its many members, just as Paul will write later in Romans 12. The practical recognition of the dignity of each person comprises faithful proclamation of Christ's death in the worship gathering and shapes how believers are to live until he comes again (v. 26).[15] Paul's explanation of the liturgical tradition amounts to an exhortation that the community be more authentically what they are called to be or, as Augustine later put it, that they become the body that they receive, the sacrament of the peace and unity achieved by Christ.[16]

But while the substance of the eucharistic tradition as a fraternal sharing perdured from the apostolic period through Justin up to and with Augustine, the ritual form of its practice changed during those ensuing centuries, and inevitably so, it would seem, due to the exponential growth in Church membership by the early fifth century. Gathering around the table of a shared meal in house churches morphed into processing to the front of the basilica to receive the body of Christ from the ordained minister. Bernard Cooke's comprehensive thesis for a threefold (philosophical, hierarchical, and ritual) distancing from the God experientially shared by the first generations of believers in Christ gathering momentum by the fourth century is borne out here by the fact that fewer and fewer baptized members of the church joined the Communion procession at all.[17] This is a complex history, of course, but some attention to the procession and reception of Communion down the ages (a method Robert Taft promoted)[18] can be instructive about the social and thus ecclesial perceptions of human dignity, active membership in the Church as Christ's body, and assurance of salvation/redemption in comparison and contrast to our contemporary situation.

---

15. On the performative character of proclamation (*kataggelete*), see Morrill, "Struggle," 70.

16. See Tillard, *Flesh*, 40, 42.

17. See Cooke, *Distancing*, 37–56.

18. See Taft, "Structural," 314–29.

Offering and Communion Processions: A Historical Survey

In his historical survey of fourth to eighth century eucharistic rituals, sermons, and practices, Robert Cabié highlights two types of practices whereby the faithful who came forward for Communion maintained the identification of their lives with that of Christ, as well as with the lives of their fellow assembled believers. One was the requirement that all communicants bring food from their tables at home to present to the ministers, portions of which (bread and wine) would be designated for eucharistic Communion while the rest would be used to feed the poor and the clergy. The dignity entailed in the donation is evident in the oft-repeated reminder of the Council of Elvira (ca. 300) that the bishop should receive such offerings only from those who would be sharing in the Communion Rite.[19] Homiletic evidence across several centuries and regions indicates that the rich were not to communicate in the Eucharist at the expense of the poor. While the actual means of delivery ranged from an unremarkable depositing of the gifts in the sacristy in Gaul to the hymned and incensed clerical procession with the people prostrating as the gifts passed in the churches of the East (the origins of the Orthodox "Great Entrance"), another type of procession developed in Africa and acquired detailed description in the Roman *Ordo I*: At the beginning of the liturgy of the Eucharist, the people brought their offerings—bread and wine, food and tithes—forward to the ministers before or even up to the altar table. Thus, the liturgy entailed two processions of the people, accompanied by psalms with antiphons, one for bringing forth the fruits of human labor and the other for receiving the mystical body of the Lord. Cabié recounts, "St. Augustine sees in this double procession an expression of the 'marvelous exchange' represented by the incarnation: Christ takes our humanity in order to bestow on us his divinity."[20]

I want to pause here to note that such a theological reality comes only (to echo Louis-Marie Chauvet)[21] at the mercy of the body, that is, the divine grace comes only through the anthropologically powerful experience of processing amidst a specially assembled body of people. Allow me to fast-forward (fast!) to the present, to one performance of the post-Vatican II liturgy, the outcome of the council's radical reorienting of the Mass as an

---

19. See Cabié, *Eucharist*, 82.
20. Cabié, *Eucharist*, 78.
21. See Chauvet, *Sacraments*, xii.

active participation in the Christ's paschal mystery, as opposed to the post-Tridentine gazing at the transubstantiated host so as to receive something of the "fruits" of the clerically executed and consumed Blessed Sacrament. The objective of the reform (putting in official motion that of the Liturgical Movement) was to recover the full engagement of all in the liturgy, as enactors of the ritual symbolism, the source and summit of the people's ongoing lives as the ethical, social, and interpersonal work of human sanctification, of salvation. Such realization of the gospel in the practical workings of the world is, according to primordial Christian tradition, the very glory of God.

My story must be brief: In 1994, I visited Loyola University of New Orleans for some days of relaxation between writing doctoral dissertation chapters. To my Sunday morning inquiry about a good place to go to Mass, the guys in the Jesuit dining room recommended the parish in one of the city's poorest, most troubled neighborhoods. I made my way there, parked my car amidst the broken glass of the street, and joined the almost entirely African-American congregation for what proved an exuberant two-hour liturgy combining the Mass of Paul VI with the music, bodily and vocal prayer styles, and preaching patterns of African-American Christianity. Most arresting and memorable for me were the two processions of the entire assembly framing the Liturgy of the Eucharist, which began with every member—old and young, women, men, and children—coming up the main aisle to deposit their donations in a large basket at the foot of the altar, singing and dancing with the choir's anthem. Bringing up the rear were elders and children bearing bread and wine. I was witnessing the type of procession I had read about in Cabié's historical study. And I was floored, especially as I experienced the impact on the second procession for Communion, how much more communal and consecratory and empowering it felt due to its mirroring the first corporate movement. The proclamation of Christ in the word—of the Jesus tempted by Satan yet triumphant in sticking to God's ways (for it was the First Sunday of Lent)—became written on the bodies of all Christ's members, whose identification with him they expressed in the twofold procession pattern. I do not mean to romanticize that congregation in their dignity amidst the poverty of racism, drug violence, and so forth. But the revelatory character and impact of that liturgy for those participants, in the myriad joys and concerns they'd brought and convictions of purpose they took away, seemed undeniable. And I would argue that, however somatically bland the single Communion processions in the Anglo-American Catholic parishes may be in contrast, still, the act of processing, one by one amidst a ritual body as one, writes a deep, poly-valent, uniquely personal message on the bodies of all. The robust practices Latinos are bringing to US Catholicism, of course, would provide much for further reflection on procession.[22]

But how did that get lost? Back to our historical survey we return: By the ninth century, in the Latin churches the people's donations from their own tables was fading fast and then vanished with theologians' con-demnations of the use of leavened bread for the Eucharist. The procession disappeared, and the preparation of the gifts became the provenance of the clergy in the sanctuary, one of many factors by the tenth century contrib-uting to the decline in the people's participation in the Eucharist. As for the Communion procession, Cabié reports, "As a matter of fact, at a very early period the faithful fell into the habit of approaching the Lord's table only rarely, and it was judged better to let non-communicants leave" after the Lord's Prayer and before the fraction rite.[23] In sixth-century Gaul, Cae-sarius of Arles ordered that the faithful stay until the Our Father and then receive a blessing, while Gregory of Tours spoke of the Communion Rite occurring "after the dismissal." That tripartite blessing/dismissal remained a widespread practice through the Middle Ages, and it aligns with the re-peated evidence that Communion by the laity was a rarity. When twelfth-century theologians and mystics led revivals of lay Communion at Mass, the clergy had no idea how to minister the sacrament in the context of a regular parish Mass, so that liturgists "then had recourse to [inserting] the ritual used in communion of the sick."[24] With rare, scattered exceptions, any ritual vestiges of the Mass as *communio*, as fraternal sharing foster-ing fraternal charity, and, thus, of the Eucharist as a corporate, communal experience shaping the social-political imagination and judgments of the people, were gone.

Not that people stopped judging one another. The citizens of West-ern Christendom did so, however, by other social conventions. Cabié gives this account of the seventeenth century: "Abstention from Communion was so much a part of local mores that those who wished to communicate would do so after the crowd had gone, lest they appear to be 'flaunting themselves.'"[25] Thus developed the early morning "Communion Mass" for

22. See, for just one example, Goizueta, *Caminemos*, 102–31.

23. Cabié, *Eucharist*, 116.

24. Cabié, *Eucharist*, 167.

25. Cabié, *Eucharist*, 178.

the pious laity who could receive out of the view of the rest of the faithful, whom they would join later at the main parish Mass. Liturgical historian James White observes:

> It may seem an anomaly today, but well up into the twentieth century Communion was not normally given to the people at what is assumed to be the appropriate moment, after the Communion of the priest, but before, after, or from a side altar at any point during the Mass . . . to kneeling communicants, who interrupted their devotions during the Mass to receive from a priest not engaged in the Mass. Our sense of Communion as an integral part and climax of the community's actions would have amazed most eighteenth-century worshipers.[26]

The content and vigor of Pius X's reforming efforts for the Eucharist—his mandates for early and frequent Communion and the endorsement of the Liturgical Movement's scholarship valorizing the active participation of all the faithful in the liturgy—truly set a new course for the church's eucharistic practice in the twentieth century. To deny the revolutionary character of the Second Vatican Council's Constitution on the Sacred Liturgy seems to me to require no mean feat of rationalization, but as we know, certain clerical and lay forces in the church are hard at it. An analysis of the issues and *dramatis personae* is beyond the scope and time available to me here,[27] but elements may arise as I turn once more in conclusion to the contemporary controversies over receiving Communion as a contested site for liturgy and ethics in the US Catholic Church.

Ritual and Moral Agency in Contemporary US Catholicism

If the scandal in earlier eras was a matter of individuals having the gall to present themselves for Holy Communion at the main altar during a regular parish Mass, the conventional social and religious mores of American Catholics today run in the opposite direction. Attend just about any Mass anywhere around the United States and one will find that it is the odd person in the congregation who does *not* join in the Communion procession. So great is the individual felt need not to be left out of the communal action that pastoral ministers have had to develop for those not in "full

26. White, *Roman Catholic Worship*, 37, 61.

27. For a balanced, critical account and assessment, see Baldovin, *Reforming*, 1–12, 158–73.

communion with the Catholic Church" the ritual accommodation of cross-
ing their hands over their breast to indicate to the Communion minister
that they desire a "blessing" in place of receiving the consecrated host.
People with youngsters bring them along in the Communion line even
though they have not yet received their First Holy Communion, with the
young ones often reaching for the host the parent is receiving. The little
children's actions (their expectations that they should get a "cracker," too),
however unwittingly (or perhaps intuitively?), symbolize the attitude of
the vast majority in the assembly: "All Are Welcome" (as a widely popular
opening hymn by that title repeatedly proclaims).

Here we have a fine example of what sociologist of religion Jerome
Baggett describes as the most common interpretive practice of tradition
among US Catholics of all classes and ethnicities today: negotiation. His
summary analysis (toward the end of his relatively recent and substantial
book synthesizing extensive fieldwork, data, and scholarly sources) war-
rants quotation in full:

> An outcropping of what Michele Dillon calls the enhanced "in-
> terpretive authority" among Catholics (officially legitimated
> by Vatican II), negotiating with the broader tradition basically
> means appropriating those meanings proper to it in ways that
> best coincide with one's own sense of self. People speak of "my
> faith" because, aware of the religious agency they have grown ac-
> customed to exercising, they think of their religious identity as a
> product of their past choices and future goals, both of which can
> be quite individualized. Cognizant that others have made differ-
> ent choices and mapped out dissimilar life goals, they highlight
> their nonjudgmentalism and religious unknowing by refusing to
> enter the tabernacle of ultimate "Truth" and preferring instead to
> linger within the outer portico of what is true "for me." Less sure
> of what they know, they tend to focus on how they act as a means
> of identifying themselves as Catholic, and they then monitor their
> actions to determine whether they are (or are likely to become) a
> "good person." Finally, they undertake this negotiation process in
> conjunction with—often in resistance to—an institutional church
> that, while generally setting the parameters of their religious agen-
> cy, most parishioners understand as simultaneously necessary and
> fraught with serious shortcomings.[28]

28. Baggett, *Sense*, 216.

Baggett immediately continues his next paragraph: "These themes appear again and again as Catholics go about rooting themselves within their tradition in a way that feels authentic to them."[29] Although Baggett at no point considers it in his own descriptions and analyses, the Communion procession strikes me as a particularly powerful ritual-symbolic practice of what he identifies as the "tolerant traditionalism" characterizing a vast majority of American Catholics—a highly individualistic, constructive clinging to the faith while purposely refraining from judging the faith of others.[30] The now ubiquitous popular approach to the Communion procession, I would aver, enacts publicly that highly personalized, mutually accepting manner of belief, the ethos of the "people's church" that collides head on with that of the "bureaucratic church" of the clerical hierarchy, which church historian Jay Dolan observes as seemingly "ever more intent on imposing discipline and exerting control over the faithful."[31]

The hierarchy perceive the sacraments—but really, the Eucharist predominates here—as means of grace for the benefit of those who are in the state of grace, that is, with no awareness of having committed gravely immoral acts that are the matter for discerning serious sin within the Rite of Penance. Since 1973, the US Catholic bishops have made abortion the singular, nonnegotiable moral issue taking precedent over all others in society,[32] with Pope John Paul II advancing this same singularity of abortion's evil in his encyclical *Evangelium Vitae*.[33] Not surprising, then, are the public prohibitions from Communion that the most institutionally rigorous US bishops decree against Catholic politicians who support legal abortion. Not surprising, either, given the late-modern ambiguity between public and private, are the seemingly contradictory explanations the bishops tend to give in their press releases, asserting that the matter of presenting oneself for Holy Communion is a personal affair and a private matter the bishop is addressing only to the politician for the sake of his or her soul—even as he makes it a cause célèbre in his diocesan newspaper and the wider, exponentially more powerful organs of the commercial news media. Not surprising, finally is the reticence of the large majority of US Catholics to judge these politicians or anybody else for joining in the

29. Baggett, *Sense*, 216.

30. See Baggett, *Sense*, 235.

31. Baggett, *Sense*, 238.

32. See Sammon, "Politics," 11–26.

33. See John Paul II, *Evangelium Vitae*, no. 58.

Communion procession, nor the vitriolic clamor of the small but highly vocal ultra-conservative Catholics whose integralist-traditional approach to the religion sees, in these publicized issues of ethics and belief, genuine scandal and controversy. With absolutely no intention of sarcasm here, I ask whether and how the act of processing to and receiving Holy Communion in a church or cathedral can be parsed into private and public components. This honest question returns us to the very nature of the Catholic Church's reformed liturgy itself, in the structure and form and content of which the theologians of the Liturgical Movement intended to renew the engaged participation of all so as to empower their putting the faith they experience in the ritual to work in the world their baptisms have charged them to cultivate and serve.

The "bureaucratic church," to employ Dolan's terminology, insists upon proper moral and doctrinal self-examination as the ethical obligation *prior to* approaching the Eucharist, with the nearly singular doctrinal matter being a certain conceptualization of the real presence of Christ in the host—yet another contested issue worrisome to the bishops since at least the early 1990s, when a poorly worded (in my judgment) *New York Times* poll found the majority of US Catholics choosing a "symbolic" understanding of the eucharistic elements. The "popular church," in contrast, seems largely to consider *participation in* the liturgy itself as the ethically—or better yet, as Wannenwetsch argues, the ethico-politically—formative experience during which the members of Christ's body, the church, encounter their Lord in assembly, presiding minister, word, and sacrament.[34] That Sunday Mass now tends to last an hour that is evenly divided between the Liturgy of the Word and the Liturgy of the Eucharist would seem to be a reality that, over time, has tacitly brought about a significantly reflexive engagement[35] with Scripture for those who attend regularly. Even though homiletic preaching started from scratch in the late-1960s and has yet to gain a satisfactory level of quality (according to all ongoing polling data of practicing Catholics), still, it seems that the people's hearing the full complement of all four canonical Gospels over the three-year lectionary cycle and annual Easter cycle has been a significant practice affecting how they imagine and bodily approach the eucharistic table. Over the years, people hear accounts of Jesus feeding hungry multitudes, receiving criticism for

---

34. Paul VI, *Sacrosanctum Concilium*, no. 7.

35. For a discussion of how the social theory of reflexivity informs late-modern Catholics' approach to tradition, see Baggett, *Sense*, 231–37.

dining with sinners, suffering remonstration from his own disciples for allowing a penitent woman to bathe and anoint his feet at table, and telling parables depicting the reign of God as a banquet populated by social outcasts and nobodies. Over and again, when I find myself in conversations with the faithful about access to Holy Communion, including the folks at Holy Spirit parish in Atlanta years ago, I am consoled to hear them readily and easily referring to those stories and images of their Lord with great conviction (which Baggett identifies as contemporary US Catholics' original negotiation and innovative working with the Bible, among several of the religion's key traditional resources).[36] This cannot but be a vital sign of a faith in good health, because practically engaged, regularly exercised.

Conclusion

On the other hand, and in conclusion, American Catholics' religious nonjudgmental attitude coupled with staunch resistance to "whatever influence the church might have in controlling people through fear and guilt" or "being 'told what to do,'" is, as Baggett himself acknowledges, troubling:

> That is, if the "good news" truly is simply a freedom to reject even the most carefully discerned judgments that conclude "this is right and this is wrong," then this may ultimately prove disempowering to church communities by undermining their capacity for meaningful ethical deliberation and consensus building.[37]

Toward the end of the carefully argued conclusion to his book, Baggett perceptively recognizes that the way American Catholics, as Americans, struggle with their ethical-religious questions is in terms of the individual self:

> How does one determine what is most authentic to oneself? How can one come to some certainty when adjudicating between what the institution should carry on and what it should cast aside? How

36. "[Catholics] rely heavily on the cultural tools handed down to them by their tradition when reflecting on the world around them. They draw from the Bible, church teachings, priests' homilies, and conversations with people they trust" in making "judgments about which doctrines are central or peripheral to the faith, which symbols seem meaningful or calcified, which features of the institutional church merit their devotion or disdain, and which aspects of the surrounding world are sacred or profane." Baggett, *Sense*, 233.

37. Baggett, *Sense*, 220.

good does one have to be to be good? In addition to cultivating tolerance, how does one truly understand the value of being Catholic and devoted to Christ in a religiously pluralist world?[38]

Telling to this liturgical theologian, nonetheless, is the way, at least to my reading, sociologist Baggett does not include the liturgy as a key traditional source—indeed, I would argue, the very site—for creatively and productively bridging the divide between modern autonomous individuality and modern rhetoric and yearning for a communal, ethically transforming experience (practice) of church. His research methods, questions, and conclusions run along the lines of individuals wrestling with biblical and doctrinal material as texts to study and discuss. I am arguing, however, that the experientially, practically different medium of engaging those sources in the liturgy, as Wannenwetsch, as well as many liturgical theologians have argued, is the practice wherein the faithful, however unevenly or inarticulately or increasingly only occasionally, continue to work out the meeting of gospel and lived convictions *in the company of others purposefully assembled in the presence of Christ.* Elsewhere, I have written on the resistance of American Catholics, including many of the ordained, to engage the significant amount of prophetic and judgment-oriented texts that appear annually in the liturgical year's lectionary cycle (widely choosing, for example, excruciatingly banal songs irrelevant to the proper seasons).[39] I end here only able to acknowledge the complexity of the phenomenon that liturgy as ritual is, but with the conviction that scholarly study of such elements as the Communion procession, examined in synchronic and diachronic ritual and contextual detail, promises descriptive and prescriptive contributions liturgical theology can offer a rapidly, drastically changing Church.

38. Baggett, *Sense*, 236.
39. See Morrill, "Beginning," 65–74.

4

Penance

Differing Views of Power, Ecclesial and Sacramental

Introduction

FULFILLING THE SECOND VATICAN Council's mandate for a revision of the "rite and formulas for the sacrament of penance" that would "more clearly express both the nature and effect of the sacrament,"[1] the Congregation for Divine Worship decreed implementation of the reformed Rite of Penance on December 2, 1973. Whereas the Council's directive in *Sacrosanctum Concilium* was so succinct as to comprise all of one sentence, the decree and introduction to the new Rite of Penance were, characteristically, thorough in articulating a theology for the practice, including the Church's primordial, dominical, evangelical duty to proclaim repentance, "calling the faithful to continual conversion and renewal."[2] Yet already in the 1960s, the practice of confession was in significant decline in many parts of the world, such that by the time implementation of the approved English translation of the rite in the United States was underway in the mid-1970s, the (to this day) pop cultural Catholic image of the Saturday afternoon and evening confessional lines was largely a memory. Historian James O'Toole recounts

1. Paul VI, *Sacrosanctum Concilium*, no. 72.
2. "Rite of Penance," 534; see also no. 1.

how "in the mid-1960s, confession seemed to disappear almost completely from the fiber of Catholic identity and custom. . . . Practically overnight, the lines of Saturday afternoons vanished and the hours appointed for confession dwindled as even the most ardent Catholics stayed away."[3] Ten years after Pope Paul VI's approval of the revised Rite of Penance, Pope John Paul II in 1983 convened the Sixth General Assembly of the Synod of Bishops to discuss the related themes of reconciliation and penance, a topic that numerous bishops from around the globe had suggested with concern not only for the Church's broad mission of reconciliation (*ad intra* and *ad extra*) but moreover with special urgency for what they assessed to be the troubled state of the sacrament of penance among both laity and clergy.[4]

Meanwhile, during that heady period of studying and implementing the full panoply of renewed ecclesial rites, North American sacramental-liturgical theologians were publishing an impressive complement of articles and books, which clergy, religious, and burgeoning ranks of engaged laity read singly and in academic courses and summer institutes across the continent. Publisher Michael Glazier enlisted Monica Hellwig to edit their Message of the Sacraments series, producing in the early 1980s books on each of the seven sacraments plus a volume on sacraments in general. Prominent among the objectives each author was to pursue was an accounting of "the existential or experiential meaning of the sacrament in the context of secular human experience," as well as "a theological exposition of the meaning, function and effect of the sacrament in the context of present official Catholic doctrinal positions."[5] The work was to mine history while being mindful of contemporary pastoral needs. In her preface for the series, Hellwig presented the volumes as serving the church "at a critical juncture in its history . . . a trying and often frustrating time for those most interested in the life of the Church and most deeply committed to it," including the series' authors, who had "undertaken the study [with] sober optimism."[6] Notable among them were Nathan Mitchell's on the sacrament of order, James Empereur's on anointing of the sick,[7] and, arguably most impressive of all, Hellwig's contribution on penance. Her *Sign of Reconciliation and Conversion: The Sacrament of Penance for Our Times* appeared just

---

3. O'Toole, "Hear No Evil." See also Tentler, "Souls," 291, 306–7.

4. See John Paul II, *Reconciliation*, no. 4.

5. Hellwig, *Sign*, vii.

6. Hellwig, *Sign*, viii.

7. See Mitchell, *Mission*; and Empereur, *Prophetic Anointing*.

a little over one year prior to John Paul's convening of that episcopal synod in October 1983.

Hellwig's is an exemplary work in sacramental theology, achieving in just little over 150 lucid pages a beautiful integration of the pastoral, theological, and historical due to the clarity of the fundamental insights she pursued with compassion for the contemporary faithful in a time of great anthropological and, thus, practical-ecclesiological change. Reading Scripture and tradition historically with a view to what conversion (with its cognate, repentance), reconciliation, and penance might mean now for the faithful—personally, interpersonally, and communally—she hit all the right pastoral (and thus, theological) notes. Reading in tandem John Paul's 1984 post-synodal letter, *Reconciliation and Penance*, one cannot but be struck by how prominently the same categories of reconciliation, conversion, and repentance shape the composition and yet, ultimately, come together in a significantly different—and at moments, discordant—key from Hellwig's composition.

This chapter will first review Hellwig's sacramental theology of conversion with a view to how she perceives power—not only divine but also human, between clergy, religious, and laity—to be at work in practices of repentance and reconciliation. Then shall follow a comparison and contrast of the theological hermeneutics of history, ecclesial authority, and practice in John Paul's apostolic exhortation, *Reconciliation and Penance*. Theological analysis of those two texts will lead to consideration of history, both the two author's contrasting methodological approaches to history and the historical context of their writing, that is, the "world behind" their texts. The context has in the ensuing decades only become more contested as to understandings and practices of ecclesial, sacramental, and anthropological (individual and communal) power. I shall end with a practical theological suggestion for the ritual impasse at which North American (and much of global) Catholicism has arrived with regard to the sacrament of penance and rites of reconciliation. This is a matter of second-order theology arising from and returning to first-order theology, of symbol giving rise to thought, and thought returning to symbol. Such hermeneutical circling, such integration of theory and practice, is essential to good sacramental-liturgical theology, which methodological principle I hope to demonstrate in my critical-to-constructive conclusion.

Hellwig's Sign of Reconciliation and Conversion

For Hellwig, the entirety of the Church's mission is the "practical task" of "facilitating conversions."[8] Elaboration on that initial thesis lays the foundation for all she theologically argues and historically rehearses through the remainder of the book:

> More fundamental than any of the obviously religious or "churchy" activities, more fundamental than hierarchic or clerical functions, more fundamental than institutional unity and doctrinal orthodoxy and continuity, is the task of being community, the task of a genuine, practical, far-reaching sharing of life and resources and ideals and mutual respect and support. This is the basic channel by which the grace of God is communicated and becomes effective in rescuing each of us and all of us from our alienation, reconciling us with our true source and goal and center which is God (2 Cor. 5:16–21).[9]

That clear assertion about the nature of God's grace as situated in human communion, in addition to her description of the paradoxical and illusive nature of sin as asking "for a far more radical faith and trust than most of us are ready to make for most of our lives,"[10] shapes the way Hellwig reads the New Testament and Christian origins. Locating the church's meaning and purpose in the person of Christ Jesus, "and not in the light of any codifiable law," she characterizes life "under the impulse of the Spirit" as a lifelong maturation of faith in each believer, as well as a "centuries long, continuing and unending journey of discovery for the church,"[11] which church she consistently identifies with the body of all the baptized sharing through word (Scripture, stories, doctrines) and sacrament (symbols and rituals). The priority for interpreting the history and present practices of reconciliation and conversion, therefore, lies with the church's evangelical mission, and all aspects of polity must answer to it. As such, Hellwig's theology is notably representative of the methodologies of *réssourcement*, the New Theology, and Liturgical Movement that altogether found validation in Vatican II, implementation through the Consilium's revision of all the rites, scholarly dissemination internationally through the writings of

---

8. Hellwig, *Sign*, 23.

9. Hellwig, *Sign*, 23–24.

10. Hellwig, *Sign*, 22.

11. Hellwig, *Sign*, 23.

Schillebeeckx and Rahner, and in North America through the educational and popular writing achievements of herself and such colleagues as Bernard Cooke and Gerard Sloyan.[12]

Theological Enlistment of History

Hellwig's four-chapter historical survey of Christian repentance and conversion follows the widely accepted two-stage pattern characterizing, first, the patristic era in terms of public canonical penance (*exomologesis*), which gradually collapsed as a second pastoral-ritual process developed in the form of private confessions to monks and, by the end of the first millennium, to priests.[13] Elements of both types finally merged during the medieval period into the sacrament of confession as prescribed at the Fourth Lateran Council and later confirmed by the Council of Trent, such that auricular confession submitting to the judgment of a sin-absolving priest remains the official, mandatory form of penance to this day. Hellwig rehearses that history so as to arrive at "one point" she asserts is "quite clear," namely, that since "the community has in the past developed the rites according to the needs of the times, therefore it can assuredly continue to do this in the present and future."[14] That conviction, coupled with her pastoral passion for the church as "the great inclusive sacrament of repentance . . . co-extensive with that totality of ['secular'] life together,"[15] shapes her theology of the sacrament, past and present, its efficacy, and then her assessment of current problems, not the least of which is a too narrow identification of sacramental grace with clerical ritual, of reconciliation and repentance with auricular confession.

Hellwig's theological method, then, is to read history with an eye to variety, contestation, change, and evolution, and all of this not so as to find amidst (or worse yet, despite) the details, the red thread of some inerrant constancy of ideology and practice but rather, to the contrary, to flesh out in the eschatologically tense body of Christ the strengths and weaknesses, advances and setbacks in the church's life that *is* an ongoing conversion. The subjects of Christian conversion, then, are not only individual believers but

12. See Carey, "Two Pioneers," 223–47.

13. For other historical studies, see Favazza, *Order*; Dallen, *Reconciling Community*, 1–201; and Kidder, *Making Confession*, 1–189.

14. Hellwig, *Sign*, 62.

15. Hellwig, *Sign*, 29.

also the church—leaders and laity, in doctrine and practice—in particular places and successive eras. The power and assurance of graced mission in the vicissitudes of history is the Spirit of the One who raised Jesus from the dead.

The *anamnesis* performed especially in the Eucharist Hellwig situates front and center in her treatment of the first quarter of Christian history, for it manifested amidst the assembly of the baptized each Lord's Day the divine grace of repentance and reconciliation fundamental to the long, slow, gradual conversion tacitly characteristic of daily Christian life. Augustine's writings attest to thrice-daily recitation of the Lord's Prayer and constant acts of charity as characteristic of that quotidian ecclesial life of reconciliation and conversion. He also, among others, recounts the pattern, purpose, and cause for what had become canonical public penance—*exomologesis*—the Church's way for dealing with the serious, capital sins of apostasy, adultery (or fornication), and murder. Hellwig is quick to point out the typical translation of *exomologesis* as "confession" can be deceiving if anachronistically understood to imply simple confession of specific sins directly to a priest (which in that era would largely have been the bishop). In fact, Tertullian, Cyprian, Leo the Great, and others employ the term to describe a lengthy, rigorous public ritual process of prayer, fasting, almsgiving, and symbolic penitential gestures to be performed not only by the capital sinner but also the minister and peoples at times with them. The process culminated in the bishop's publicly laying hands on the penitent as the sign of readmission to the Eucharist, a ritual event that generally became situated on Maundy Thursday. As for actual articulation of sin(s) committed, Pope Leo (mid-fifth century) made it clear this should not be a public act, whether verbal or written but, rather, part of a "secret" discussion with the priestly minister.[16] Leo also describes what other patristic texts attest, as well; namely, that the exercise of power by the bishop (or perhaps, in the case of very large dioceses, a priest) was one of intercessory prayer *to* God *on behalf of* the penitent.

16. Hellwig, *Sign*, 39. James Dallen, likewise noting Leo's letter of 459, provides this explanation: "In one sense, confession was private, insofar as counseling is concerned (though when it became customary is conjecture), but the significant confession was public: the *exomologesis* by which the penitent heard and responded to the call to conversion and confessed the One whose merciful love had brought salvation to the sinner. Confession for the ancient Church was praising God for compassion to the sinner. The returning sinner's meeting with the bishop was no more and no less than the pastoral counseling that such a person would seek and receive today." Dallen, *Reconciling Community*, 67.

The meritorious feature of canonical penance in the first five-to-six centuries of the Church, Hellwig avers, was its strongly communal, ecclesial, corporate character:

> To sin is always to damage the fabric of the community and cause rifts that call for reconciliations within the community. Moreover the sin of each is the responsibility of all. The work of repentance and reconciliation is the work of the whole community. All must pray and mourn and fast for the sins that break the fabric of the community and all must mediate the possibilities of repentance and conversions for one another.[17]

The ritual process, dramatic as it was, however, had so many serious flaws that its collapse into desuetude proved inevitable. The principal fault lay with the narrow list of three capital sins that, nonetheless when focused exclusively on individual acts, ignored the wider social body's accountability for their occurrence and, with that, others' tacit complicity through related harmful actions, practices, and social conventions. Plus, the penalties were so severe—especially the requirement of lifelong celibacy for sins against chastity—that people avoided *exomologesis* while still publicly receiving Holy Communion. For Hellwig, the key fault laid in a rigid distinction between saints and sinners that flagrantly contradicted the gospel message at the heart of the church's life, namely, "the ongoing need of conversion for all."[18] For those reasons, Hellwig judges as inevitable the emergence of new forms of penance and reconciliation suitable to the Church's mission of being the sign of reconciliation and conversion in the world.

Salutary was the Celtic practice of confessing sins in the course of individuals' seeking counsel with monks, both male and female, whose very way of life was "voluntary penitence in the quest for perfection."[19] In that context, the practical understanding of penance was in terms not "of guilt and expiation" but "of woundedness and healing," and the role of the monastic confessor, not of sentencing judge but of compassionate discerner, pleading to God with and on behalf of the penitent.[20] Such practices came to flourish in the Celtic and British Isles, then spread back onto the Continent

---

17. She adds, "This sense of corporate involvement tended to disappear with the gradual disuse of canonical penance, though there are remnants of its survival in the celebration of Lent, Advent, Ember and Rogations days." Hellwig, *Sign*, 65–66.

18. Hellwig, *Sign*, 45.

19. Hellwig, *Sign*, 66.

20. Hellwig, *Sign*, 67.

where, by the ninth century, private confessions to priests of all but the most notorious, egregious acts was becoming widespread. While synods advanced the convention of private confession they, nonetheless, left to the priest-confessor both criteria for judgment of sin and the penance to be assigned. In that official vacuum developed priests' penitential books, indexing sins and their tariffs, the private and arbitrary (thus, unofficial) qualities of which bishops opposed. By the turn of the second millennium, the heavy tariffs had ceded to decreasingly severe penances, and those increasingly to be performed *after* the priest-confessor declared the penitent reconciled. With all of that and more came increased regular confession of less grave sins, especially during Lent and in relation to Easter Communion.

Lateran IV's mandate of the "Easter Duty" in 1215, then, was not a new invention. Hellwig assesses the resultant sacrament of penance to be a merger of some of the better qualities of both the earlier traditions, canonical and monastic. Notable, however, among that council's regulations for confession, and reinforced at Trent in 1515, was approbation, "almost without any discussion or critical reflection,"[21] of the formula of forgiveness having changed from the minister's intercessory prayer *to* God for the penitent to his *declaring* sins forgiven *in the name of* God. The unequivocal identification of the Church's power to forgive sins with the power of office, through priestly ordination, and jurisdiction, through episcopal assignments of their priests to parishes and eventually of religious priests' faculties within their dioceses—clerical power in force to this day—had consequences Hellwig articulates with pastoral passion:

> Those who, as in former times, are deeply experienced in the life of the Spirit and have a special charism for reconciliation and conversion of others are now very distinctly barred from the ministry of sacramental or ecclesial reconciliation if they are women or unordained men. Their ministry of guiding others through a conversion, while in itself perhaps deeply and far-reachingly effective, as in the case of Catherine of Siena, for instance, simply "does not count."[22]

Therein lies the power struggle—human and divine, the faithful and the Holy Spirit[23]—that Hellwig reads throughout the history of the Church,

21. Hellwig, *Sign*, 73.

22. Hellwig, *Sign*, 74.

23. "In many ways, therefore, the living Spirit in the living Church simply could not be confined within the ironclad system described in the ruling of the Fourth Lateran Council." Hellwig, *Sign*, 75.

finding in the monastic centers and eventual mendicant friars (even later, one might add, the Jesuits and other religious) divine provision for the needs of the baptized, "a practical implementation [of the sacrament of penance] that was more human, more personal, more concerned with conversion."[24] The dangerous powers menacing the Rite of Penance included a juridical tenor of "court process, judgment and sentence" that, tragically, inverted the priority of spiritual direction and confession of sin and, with that, reduced the latter to rote lists of offenses complemented by conventional penances of memorized prayers.

Ministry to Conversions: Official Rites and Communal Charismata

In contrast to routinized recitation of sins in the confessional, Hellwig desires that *genuine* conversion—she does not prescind from such adjectives, quite the opposite[25]—be fostered and, thus, the authentically evangelical life of the Church, in its members, to flourish. Turning her analysis to the reformed Rite of Penance (1973) in its provision of three ritual forms,[26] she places much hope and promise in the third form, with its communal celebration of word, prayer, and general sacramental absolution, even as she notes its being "hemmed about with many restrictions."[27] And at this point, I must switch verb tenses from the present (of her text) to the past (of its historical situation). For Hellwig's insightful observation of what at the end of the twentieth century the vast majority of Roman Catholics who had abandoned auricular confession needed—that they "be challenged not to forget the constant need for discernment of what is sinful and what is redemptive in the world and in one's own life and . . . offered help in that

24. Hellwig, *Sign*, 76.

25. This reader found himself tracking, as the book advanced, the modifiers pervading Hellwig's rhetoric of conversion. Conversion may be: true, continuing, genuine, real, deeper, particular, communal, universally needed, inner, or integral. See Hellwig, *Sign*, 74, 77, 79, 80, 86, 91, 95, 108, 111, 118. All such terms, of course, imply the possibility of the opposite qualities (faux conversions, perhaps, or the lack of any conversion at all in mere rote recitations of standard faults and sins, followed by perfunctory prayers prescribed as penance) being operative in individuals, a local community, or even the wider Church at any historical moment.

26. These include: (1) Rite for Reconciliation of Individual Penitents; (2) Rite for Reconciliation of Several Penitents with Individual Confession and Absolution; and (3) Rite for Reconciliation of Penitents with General Confession and Absolution. See "Rite of Penance," nos. 15–35.

27. Hellwig, *Sign*, 82.

discernment"[28]—and her candid assessment that for many (indeed, the growing majority) this was all they were willing to accept, was altogether indicative of her hopeful expectation that the Holy Spirit would guide the leadership of the Church themselves to discern further changes in sacramental practices and canonical regulation of penance.

Hellwig did not downplay the crisis that had beset the first form of the Rite (auricular confession), listing the laity's responses to it as ranging from the majority's outright abandonment of it to a troubled small minority's "unwillingness to drop the practice while nevertheless unable to make any sense of it."[29] Extensive interviews in the years immediately after the implementation of the revised Rite of Penance found that even those still feeling obligated to go to confession largely had "concluded that sacramental penance does not make any difference," making it "a sign of something that it does not effect," comprised of contrived lists of sins, prescribed prayers, and an abrupt absolution.[30] If that was the way the laity had gone, however, the hierarchy responded in a fashion quite contrary to Hellwig's optimism that communal rites of reconciliation, serving the people's affinity for hearing in common the biblical word of repentance and conversion and sacramental word of forgiveness, might be allowed to flourish while leaving individual needs for support and encouragement to be met by "that kind of lay and mutual confession that takes place over the kitchen table between neighbors and friends."[31] Likening the dynamic to that of earlier Christians seeking counsel and confession from monks and anchorites, she adds:

> Many women who are quiet centers and anchors in their own homes have special gifts of healing, discernment, calling to repentance and reconciliation. In an unofficial and utterly unpretentious way there are many little domestic churches where a basic and authentic ministry of reconciliation and conversion is going on.[32]

28. Hellwig, *Sign*, 82.

29. Hellwig, *Sign*, 106.

30. Hellwig, *Sign*, 106. Historian James O'Toole likewise gives an account of how both US Catholic laity and clergy became dissatisfied with how "the perfunctory nature of the encounter [of priest and penitent] lent an air of the assembly line to confessional practice," with the growth of popular psychology and broaden awareness of the social and interpersonal dimensions of sin compounding disaffection with auricular confession. O'Toole, "Hear No Evil."

31. Hellwig, *Sign*, 111–12.

32. Hellwig, *Sign*, 112.

Thus does she situate the power of such ministry in (unofficial) charismata, rather than (official) sacramental orders. In contrast, the Sixth Synod of Bishops, convened almost immediately after the publication of Hellwig's book, resulted in a lengthy papal exhortation that read history with a different hermeneutics of power, charting a way forward closed to modification of official rites and, seemingly, to the ways the Holy Spirit might be speaking through voices other than the Roman magisterium.

John Paul II's Reconciliation and Penance

In his post-synodal exhortation *Reconciliation and Penance*, Pope John Paul II acknowledges early and often the troubled state of penance in the life of the Church. That he and the synod of bishops perceived the problem to be of fundamental practical import is evident in the fact that fully half of the entire document is devoted to discussing the "precise ministerial functions directed toward a concrete practice of penance and reconciliation"[33]—of which auricular confession holds priority and, with it, the office of the priest. John Paul, nonetheless, situates what he calls "the means that enable the church to promote and encourage full reconciliation," in analyses of, first, the Church's "mission of reconciliation" between and among God and people and, second, "the radical cause" of all such division, "namely sin."[34] Neglect or misunderstanding of sin has come seriously to impede what the Church has to offer men and women confounded by "the ferments of good and evil"—divisions, alienations, domination, conflicts—even as people paradoxically demonstrate "an irrepressible desire for peace."[35] An array of forces—not only across societies but also, notably, within the Church itself—have resulted in an excessive and even exclusive view of the causes for division and evil behavior, as well as proposed solutions, to be attributed only to "horizontal" or "external" human factors, to the disastrous neglect of the "vertical" and "inner" ones.

---

33. John Paul II, *Reconciliation*, no. 23.

34. John Paul II, *Reconciliation*, no. 4.

35. John Paul II, *Reconciliation*, nos. 1, 3.

Doctrinally Correcting Conversion's Wayward Course

Various forms of secularism and materialism—popular, political, and philosophical—have, the pope argues, led to an inversion of the proper priority of conversion over reconciliation, such that people's scattered efforts at peace and justice fail to take lasting hold. For reconciliation has a "hidden root—reconciliation, so to speak, 'at the source,' which takes place in people's hearts and minds," if only they perceive God's healing of the wound of original sin, with all its divisiveness, by "the blood and the cross of his Son made man," God's offer of "original reconciliation."[36] Only individual conversion of heart, return to God, and personal conversion achieved through the sacraments can ground hope for overcoming divisions and realizing peace "in all sectors of society." In addition to converting such actual human agents, the sacramental practice of the Church performs a prophetic function for wider society. With the *true* meaning of reconciliation being "profoundly religious,"[37] the Church's "message and ministry of penance" must go "beyond the boundaries of . . . the community of believers," addressing "all men and women, because all need conversion and reconciliation."[38]

In all this positive content, nonetheless, the reader notes a cumulative sense, through both direct statements and indirect allusions, of what the pope and bishops perceive to have gone wrong theologically, in both theory and practice, over the preceding couple decades. Not surprisingly, John Paul's dissatisfaction with liberation theology, that is, his judgment that Marxist materialism had led to the clergy's direct involvement in socio-economic-political affairs to the abandonment of the Church's proper mission, looms large throughout the introduction and first two parts of the document. The introduction's rehearsal of conflicts and divisions includes those in the Church itself, which John Paul itemizes as not only denominational separations but also within Roman Catholicism proper, doctrinal and pastoral differences that "at times seem incurable."[39]

The upshot of Part 1's explanation of the Church's genuine task and commitment to conversion and reconciliation leads to the opening thesis in Part 2: "In the concrete circumstances of sinful humanity, in which there

---

36. John Paul II, *Reconciliation*, no. 4.

37. John Paul II, *Reconciliation*, no. 4.

38. John Paul II, *Reconciliation*, no. 13.

39. John Paul II, *Reconciliation*, no. 2.

can be no conversion without the acknowledgement of one's own sin, the church's ministry of reconciliation intervenes in each individual case with a precise penitential purpose."[40] The mystery (as inscrutable paradox) of sin, "the dark forces which, according to St. Paul, are active in the world almost to the point of ruling it,"[41] makes every sin not only personal but also social, leading John Paul to proffer that "one can speak of a communion of sin."[42] That rather stunning terminology the pope acknowledges as only analogous (to the communion of saints), but the analogical sense of things, he insists, must also apply to social sin, lest the truth that social sin is always the "accumulation and concentration of many personal sins" be lost. On that very point, in fact, John Paul launches into a paragraph-long condemnation of liberation theology's "watering down" and almost abolishing personal sin, and with it, "the moral conscience of an individual" through "an exclusive recognition of social guilt" situated in "some vague entity or anonymous collectivity such as the situation, the system, society, structures or institutions."[43] Doctrinal and pastoral troubles, moreover, reside to the north as well, not only in analogous corporate (communal) senses of sin acknowledged and assuaged in communal liturgical activity but also, notably, through false pastoral appropriations of the theological concept of fundamental option. It seems that pastoral ministers and theologians had widely come to modify the concept, which for Karl Rahner and Josef Fuchs was a "pre-thematic" category of human subjectivity,[44] into a psychological explanation of people's actions that "objectively changes or casts doubt upon the traditional concept of mortal sin."[45] Clearly, the hierarchy wished to reassert both formation of conscience and the canonical-sacramental requirements of penitents—works proper to the magisterium and local clergy—as the ecclesiastical mediation of divine forgiving power to human sinners.

40. John Paul II, *Reconciliation*, no. 13.

41. John Paul II, *Reconciliation*, no. 14.

42. John Paul II, *Reconciliation*, no. 16.

43. John Paul II, *Reconciliation*, no. 16.

44. See Fuchs, *Human Values*, 92–111; and Rahner, *Foundations*, 93–102.

45. John Paul II, *Reconciliation*, no. 17. Hellwig herself notes this phenomenon, reporting how official insistence upon the obligation to integral confession had raised among theologians, pastors, and laity a series of objections, including its resting upon an increasingly untenable notion of mortal sin and the impossibility to identify every individual act as serious sin (versus an underlying fundamental option). See Hellwig, *Sign*, 102.

John Paul concludes Part 2's rather lengthy exposition on sin with a comparatively brief assertion of Christ Jesus as the "mystery or sacrament of pietas," an awkward phrase based on 1 Timothy 3:15–16. The pope meditates on the term as "the hidden vital principle which makes the church the house of God, the pillar and bulwark of the truth . . . capable of penetrating the hidden roots of our iniquity in order to evoke in the soul a movement of conversion, in order to redeem it and set it on course toward reconciliation."[46] Scripture reveals the *mysterium pietatis* in such a way that man's intellect can respond in concrete ways to the offer of conversion and reconciliation. Relative to Hellwig's theology, John Paul's here is much more a matter of contrast than comparison. While both posit Christ as the key to conversion and reconciliation, Hellwig does so in terms of the person of Jesus, as portrayed in the Gospel narratives of his teaching, healing, and reconciling, and all of this, we should recall, to assert "being community" as the fundamental priority for the Church's work, versus any "codifiable law." John Paul, on the other hand, in identifying "Christ himself" with the arcane term *mysterium pietatis* turns to hymnic, kerygmatic Pauline and Johannine material[47] so as to rehearse dogmatic categories and mythological imagery that set up the third and final, large pastoral part of the Exhortation along the lines of hierarchy teaching and disciplining laity (and lower clergy) in matters of conversion and penance, doctrinal and sacramental.

Part Three of the document consequently opens with what one might call the classical Roman Catholic narrative[48] of a seamless transition from Christ the sacrament of pietas to the Lord's entrusting the mission of the Church to the bishops. A Church that "finds herself face to face with man . . . wounded by sin and affected by sin in the innermost depths of his being" is only able to continue the "redemptive work of her divine founder" if "it seeks to express itself in precise ministerial functions directed toward a concrete practice of penance and reconciliation."[49] The "essentials of that pastoral activity" consist of, first, dialogue and, second, catechesis, all of

---

46. John Paul II, *Reconciliation*, no. 20.

47. John Paul II, *Reconciliation*, no. 20.

48. So maintained the council fathers: "This Sacred Council, following closely in the footsteps of the First Vatican Council, with that Council teaches and declares with it that Jesus Christ, the eternal Shepherd, established His holy Church, having sent forth the apostles as He himself had been sent by the Father; and He willed that their successors, namely the bishops, should be the shepherds in his Church even to the consummation of the world." Paul VI, *Lumen Gentium*, no. 18.

49. John Paul II, *Reconciliation*, no. 23.

which should lead the faithful to regular participation in the "sacrament par excellence of penance and conversion."[50] One discovers in reading the initial section, however, that dialogue entails those sorts of activities whereby the pope and bishops work toward ecumenical reunification of the Church and resolution of divisions within Roman Catholicism and, then, through the Holy See, as advocates for peace and justice in the "wider world."[51] Dialogue, on the contrary, is not the activity proper to forming the faithful in their ongoing lives of conversion. The faithful, rather, should obediently receive from the magisterium and clergy orthodox catechesis about conversion and sin, as well as ministration of the full complement of the Church's sacraments, all of which guide them toward fruitful use of the sacrament of penance.[52]

Rescuing Confession: A Pastoral Quest Riddled with Conflicting Conversions

Space limits do not allow for a detailed rehearsal of the arguments, prescriptions, and proscriptions comprising the second and final chapter of Part 3, "The Sacrament of Penance and Reconciliation," which are lengthy. Indeed, that single chapter constitutes fully 25 percent of the entire document and, moreover, is characterized by far more specific imperatives and conclusions than all the preceding sections. This fact, in the end, indicates the pope and bishops' priority laying not so much with the array of social, global, and ecclesial activities of conversion and reconciliation as with the proper canonical and sacramental discipline expressive of the previously discussed truths all coming to bear "powerfully and clearly" on "the Catholic doctrine of the sacrament of penance."[53] Most tellingly, the introductory paragraph of this climactic chapter identifies the practical "crisis" that the synod saw for penance, with "the sacrament of confession . . . being undermined" by

50. John Paul II, *Reconciliation*, no. 23.

51. John Paul II, *Reconciliation*, no. 25.

52. The lengthy article no. 26 outlines the threefold value of penance for conversion—a change in attitudes, repentance as "a real overturning of the soul," and validation through doing penance to the point of sacrifice—before discussing some nine topics about which the faithful are in need of clarification and depth: conscience, sin, temptation, fasting, almsgiving, communion with God and people, "the concrete circumstances in which reconciliation has to be achieved" (family, community, society, creation), the four last things, and the Church's social teaching.

53. John Paul II, *Reconciliation*, no. 31.

all the forces, internal and external, rehearsed above.[54] But note: the fundamental crisis concerns not the Rite of Penance, with its three ritual forms, but rather and specifically the sacrament of *confession*. The symbolic power of that latter term, in my opinion, should not be underestimated: confession is in mortal danger.

The hierarchy's rescue plan unfolds through a half-dozen "convictions" about confession: (1) the sacrament as "the primary way of obtaining forgiveness and the remission of serious sin committed after baptism"; (2) its functions as "a kind of judicial action . . . before a tribunal of mercy," with the penitent revealing sins to the confessor and accepting from him the punishment imposed and absolution given; (3) the conditions for validity, completeness, and fruitfulness of the sacramental "sign," all of which, while a "deeply personal matter," cannot be reduced to "psychological self-liberation," but, rather, depends on the priest's power to mediate divine forgiveness; (4) "the individual and ecclesial nature" of this "intimate" sacrament as represented in "the priest by virtue of his sacred office"; (5) the "most precious result of the forgiveness obtained" in the sacrament consisting, first, of reconciliation with God but also of "the forgiven penitent . . . with himself in his inmost being, where he regains his own true identity" and thereby, with neighbor, church, and all creation; lastly and stunningly, (6) the danger to all aspects of a priest's ministry—indeed, "the whole of his priestly existence" suffering "inexorable decline"—if he "fails to receive the sacrament of penance at regular intervals."[55] There would, of course, be no need for that admonition were the synodal bishops not aware that significant numbers of priests, like the laity they served, had abandoned regular confession. From that fact, it is not difficult to assume little promotion of the sacrament by the clergy. Indeed, the pope concludes with an outright plea ("an earnest invocation") to bishops and priests to encourage greater participation in the sacrament of penance.

From that point John Paul goes on to discuss the ritual forms comprising the reformed Rite of Penance. The first form is "the only normal and ordinary way of celebrating the sacrament, and it cannot and must not be allowed to fall into disuse or be neglected."[56] One cannot help but note the desperate tone in that reiteration of the necessity of individual, integral confession; it betrays what statistical data make clear to have by the early

54. John Paul II, *Reconciliation*, no. 28.

55. John Paul II, *Reconciliation*, no. 31.

56. John Paul II, *Reconciliation*, no. 32.

1980s become a fact. The reasons given at this point, however, are of a more remedial and medicinal character than juridical, whereby the pope presses beyond the sacrament's repair of the broken state of mortal sin to its help with not only venial sins, but also such matters of "spiritual progress" as vocational discernment, spiritual apathy, and religious crisis. Such is the very stuff of spiritual direction, he observes, and such is the irreducible value of "the personal decision and commitment . . . clearly signified and promoted in this first form."[57] The great problem with all this, nonetheless, as Hellwig had already implied, is that many priests are not particularly gifted or trained for being spiritual directors. Now several decades later, despite the pope's call in this apostolic exhortation for a remarkably comprehensive formation of clergy in all aspects, human and ecclesial, of the sacrament,[58] the historical reality is that many priests and ordination candidates may not be so gifted or even so inclined.

Katarina Schuth, a leading social-scientific researcher of seminary education in the US Catholic Church, has provided analysis of statistical data and qualitative research indicating an ever-widening gap in attitudes, approaches, and practices of Catholicism between the Millennial (often called John Paul II) generation of clerics and the people, from old to young, they are assigned to serve.[59] Schuth recognizes four distinct types of religious backgrounds among the new generation of seminarians and

57. John Paul II, *Reconciliation*, no. 32.

58. After explaining "effective performance of this ministry" as dependent upon a number of "human qualities" in the confessor, along with theological, pedagogical, psychological, and biblical training plus "docility to [the Church's] magisterium," the pope asserts seminary training must include "study of dogmatic, moral, spiritual and pastoral theology (which are simply parts of a whole), but also through the study of human sciences, training in dialogue and especially in how to deal with people in the pastoral context." John Paul II, *Reconciliation*, no. 29. Still, one must wonder whether such a massive formation, even if actually offered, can be effective when the clerical culture of the seminary, plus the qualities in the actual men accepted, may not be well disposed to the enterprise in the first place.

59. Schuth reports that fully half the US Catholic population were born after Vatican II and that, furthermore, among the youngest (Millennial) cohort only 7 percent strongly identify themselves as Catholic (with 47 percent weakly self-identifying, leaving 46 percent in a medium range). This places the Millennial-generation priests in stark contrast with their peers, while their largely traditional-to-rigid appropriations of Catholicism likewise place them in tension with the middle and older generations, who maintain a more flexible view of Church teaching and practices, for which priests would be servant-leaders and guides, rather than cultic functionaries and authoritative disciplinarians. See Schuth, "Assessing," 321–23.

priests accounting for divergent senses of pastoral identity and practice. The majority of them grew up and are deeply rooted in the faith, although they split between those whose family and parish backgrounds were more progressive and those from more traditional ones who, furthermore, often participated in conservatively traditional Catholic college settings. A second sizable cohort, however, describes itself as having experienced a "major conversion." A very small proportion (6 percent) of these came from another Christian denomination, while most are baptized Catholics who, with little active church background, underwent a "reconversion" to the faith.

> These men usually have enjoyed only a short-term or sporadic association with a parish and thus lack familiarity with parish life because of the rather sudden shift in their life direction. A large number of seminarians, at least one-third, come to theological studies with this background. . . . The concern of most faculty about them is their tendency to be inflexible, overly scrupulous, and fearful. These attitudes can bring about a strict interpretation of what they think is permissible in the practice of the faith, a sense of wanting things to conform exactly to their limited experience.[60]

In addition to the "converts" and "reconverts" comprising a full third of Millennial seminarians is another 10 percent with a completely rigid understanding of the faith, whose response to their commercial, media-driven culture "is to withdraw and condemn the world as they see it. They tend to experience enormous fear—fear of change and fear of the world. . . . Such men want only clear, distinct ideas that are aligned with their view of orthodoxy."[61] Yet the spiritual direction that Pope John Paul insists is essential to the priest's role in sacramental confession entails listening, dialogue, and discernment. Notable, moreover, is the contrast in Schuth's description of the characteristics of conversion for such a sizable percentage of the rising body of clerics in the American church from the fundamental posture of reconciliation and outreach to church and world (albeit with a strong doctrine of sin) the pope expounds in the first part of his apostolic exhortation. The persistence of both Catholics and wider society associating "the Church" with the hierarchy and clergy might well raise new questions about the Church's mission as a sign of reconciliation and conversion.

The dissonance between the laity and the growing majority of their priests at such fundamental emotional, ideological, and religious levels

60. Schuth, "Assessing," 330.
61. Schuth, "Assessing," 331.

cannot but contribute to the trend Hellwig reported three decades earlier; namely, of people turning to like-minded fellow laity, whether individually or through group processes, religious or otherwise (such as prayer or Bible study groups, twelve-step and other support groups, tai chi and yoga and similar meditative practices, etc.), to work out their conversions, whether ongoing personal growth[62] or repentance in crisis, to support one another through active listening, affective companionship and solidarity, and, if so gifted, with wise advice.[63] With such practices indicative of American Catholics' desire for individual moral agency nurtured and shared with fellow believers and others of goodwill (about which, more below), the popularity of communal Advent and Lenten penance services is not difficult to understand. In contrast to entering the confessional, people are more comfortable with assembling in song and prayer, hearing together the word of God proclaimed and feeling a sense of solidarity while reflecting on sin and repentance in their own lives and, for some, even confessing serious matters to an available priest for his judgment and absolution.

Seeking Official Resolution of Confession's Crisis: Reconciling the Rites within the Rite

Indeed, in the latter disciplinary part of *Reconciliation and Penance*, John Paul writes favorably about the second form of the Rite of Penance, with its liturgy of the word and communal examination of conscience. The pope lauds the Rite for Reconciliation of Several Penitents with Individual Confession and Absolution for fostering the ecclesial character of reconciliation and conversion, while cautioning that sufficient confessors must be present so that each penitent may properly and beneficially confess all sins, both mortal and venial. Thus does the apostolic exhortation's consistent treatment of conversion and reconciliation as fundamentally inner, individual, personal, vertical—and mediated by the Church's ordained minister—reach its practical conclusion in the singular necessity of auricular confession, even when in the context of a communal rite of word and sacrament (that is, the second form of the Rite of Penance).

---

62. For a comprehensive theory, inspired by the work of Bernard Lonergan, of the Christian life as multifaceted and ongoing conversion, see Gelpi, *Committed Worship*, 1.3–55, 2.v–viii, 135–70.

63. See Hellwig, *Sign*, 110–111.

Predictable, then, is the subsequent clarification that the third (likewise communal) Rite for Reconciliation of Penitents with General Confession and Absolution is an exceptional form for extreme cases of grave necessity that "cannot become an ordinary one" and "must never lead to a lesser regard for, still less an abandonment of, the ordinary forms."[64] That detailed, clarified restriction on the proper use of the third form served to abolish the sort of pastoral possibilities Hellwig found most hopefully emerging for the implementation of the reformed Rite of Penance. That her theology, nonetheless, both in her pastoral arguments for regular use of the third form and her assessment of why regular auricular confession had reached the end of its time, was more attuned to the *sensus fidelium* (the sense of the faithful, among both laity and clergy) is evident not only in social-scientific and contemporary historical research,[65] but also by the content of several letters and allocutions warning against inappropriate uses of form three of the Rite of Penance, as well as about the dangers of confession falling into utter disuse, that the Holy See found itself obliged to issue to bishops conferences around the world years after John Paul's postsynodal apostolic exhortation.

Reconciliation and Penance concludes its correction of mistaken notions about "the freedom of pastors and the faithful to choose from among [the three] forms the one considered more suitable" by asserting that "sacraments . . . are not our property" and "consciences . . . have a right not to be left in uncertainty and confusion."[66] Sacraments and consciences are sacred, the pope emphasizes, which sacrality gives rise to the Church's establishment of laws whereby both can be served in truth. Indeed, the instructional letters addressing the contested nature and purpose of the Rite

64. John Paul II, *Reconciliation*, no. 33. To clarify: The "ordinary forms" are (1) Rite for Reconciliation of Individual Penitents, and (2) Rite for Reconciliation of Several Penitents with Individual Confession and Absolution.

65. The Center for Applied Research in the Apostolate (CARA) at Georgetown University reports the following from its 2008 scientific survey: "*Three-quarters of Catholics report that they never participate in the sacrament of Reconciliation or that they do so less than once a year*" (CARA, "Sacrament of Reconciliation," 57). More specifically, 45 percent never participate in the Rite of Penance, while 30 percent said they do so less than once a year—with that category leaving completely open the possible span of years since one's last confession. The statistics indicate, then, how small a percentage of US Catholics actually participate in celebrations of the second form of the Rite in Lent or Advent. References to the research and arguments of contemporary historians will appear in the first half of the concluding section, below.

66. John Paul II, *Reconciliation*, no. 33.

for Reconciliation of Penitents with General Absolution that the Vatican issued to the bishops of Australia (1998), Ireland (1999), and Portugal (1999), along with the subsequent, comprehensive 2000 *Circular Letter Concerning the Integrity of the Sacrament of Penance*, all invoke the authority of doctrine and the 1983 Code of Canon Law in asserting the divine institution of auricular confession with absolution, the obligation to confess all serious sins according to number and kind at least once a year, and the extremely narrow range of circumstances allowing for use of the third form of the Rite of Penance.[67] Toward its conclusion, the circular letter, quoting *Reconciliation and Penance*, judges it "foolish, as well as presumptuous . . . arbitrarily to disregard the means of grace and salvation which the Lord has provided and, in the specific case, to claim to receive forgiveness while doing without the sacrament which was instituted by Christ precisely for forgiveness."[68] And yet the persistence of such perceived folly, on the part of both laity and clergy globally, led the pope in 2002 to publish another full-scale apostolic letter in the form of a *motu proprio*, *Misericordia Dei*, to correct misunderstandings and lawless practices of the sacrament of penance.

Pope John Paul notably begins his 2002 apostolic letter by acknowledging that in the years since his 1984 post-synodal exhortation the "causes of the crisis have not disappeared," including the failure of bishops and priests, to whom he "earnestly appeal[s]" to "arm themselves with more confidence, creativity and perseverance" in promoting the sacrament of confession.[69] The pope addresses misunderstandings about the divine power for forgiveness of serious sins accessed and dispensed through the range of communal celebrations, including the Mass, and more specifically itemizes the conditions canon law allows for celebrating the third form of the Rite of Penance. Circumstances amounting to grave necessity for its celebration—a judgment reserved solely to the diocesan bishop—include an overwhelming number of the faithful facing imminent danger of death,

---

67. Congregation for Divine Worship, *Circular Letter*, nos. 1–3, 6, 7, 8, 18, 28.

68. Congregation for Divine Worship, *Circular Letter*, no. 10.

69. Laxity of commitment among the clergy would appear to motivate one of the decrees the pope found himself compelled to issue so as to shore up the "enduring efficacy" of the sacrament: "Moreover, all priests with faculties to administer the Sacrament of Penance are always to show themselves wholeheartedly disposed to administer it whenever the faithful make a reasonable request. An unwillingness to welcome the wounded sheep, and even to go out to them in order to bring them back into the fold, would be a sad sign of a lack of pastoral sensibility in those who, by priestly Ordination, must reflect the image of the Good Shepherd." John Paul II, *Misericordia Dei*, no. 1.

such as in war or natural disasters, or the geographic isolation of peoples in missionary lands, such that they have a priest available only a few days a year. Ruled out are "contrivance of situations of apparent *grave necessity*," including notions that a large number of penitents present prevents "extended pastoral conversations."[70] Those, counters the pope, "can be left to more favourable circumstances," while "a valid and worthy celebration of the Sacrament" for each penitent entails only the appropriate time needed to name the kind and number of sins committed, such that the priest can make a proper judgment on the matter presented. Worse yet would be a pastor's using the third form "because of penitents' preference for general absolution, as if this were a normal option equivalent to the two ordinary forms set out in the Ritual."[71]

The juridical obligations of both priest and penitent concerning a valid and licit confession likewise rule out what had become customary for the second form (the Rite for Reconciliation of Several Penitents with Individual Confession and Absolution) in many parts of the world; namely, restricting people to mention just one or two sins deemed representative by the penitent or generically naming only kinds of sins (thereby neglecting the obligation to state also the number).[72] The final regulation the letter sets forth is that "confessionals . . . have 'a fixed grille,' so as to permit the faithful and confessors themselves who may wish to make use of them to do so freely."[73] Such proscriptions and prescriptions point to a tension running throughout the entire corpus of Pope John Paul's letters on the sacrament of penance: priority for the juridical to the point of impersonal arrangements plus, as he himself admits, the global lack of ordained confessors,[74] that altogether undermines the pastoral paragraphs devoted to the spiritual-direction dimension of the sacrament. At the base of all this is an urgent concern for authority and power in canon law, ordained office, and formal sacrament.

---

70. John Paul II, *Misericordia Dei*, no. 4.2.e.

71. John Paul II, *Misericordia Dei*, no. 4.2.e.

72. John Paul II, *Misericordia Dei*, no. 3.

73. John Paul II, *Misericordia Dei*, no. 9.

74. John Paul II, *Misericordia Dei*, no. 4.2.b.

Theological Conclusions, Theoretical and Practical

That this present study has found a profound dissonance between the teaching and disciplinary leadership of the Roman Catholic hierarchy—identified in the present era with the Church's magisterium—and one of the leading voices among the post-Vatican II generation of American theologians is unlikely to raise many eyebrows. The purpose of this comparative exercise has been to seek greater insight into those differences by exploring two representative figures' treatments of a practical topic universally recognized as symptomatic of the change the Church has experienced since the 1960s across its hierarchical, clerical, popular, and scholarly sectors in the way power (with its cognate authority) is exercised in their practice and understanding of the faith. Crucial to the divide is the fundamental difference in theological methodology, for which this study of Hellwig's and Pope John Paul's works on penance, conversion, and reconciliation may serve as a prime, if not instructive, example. The essential methodological difference concerns the reading of history and, with that, of power and authority in the Church.

Theory for Ministry and Sacrament: History and Theology

Utterly representative of modern Catholic theological scholarship, Hellwig studies history with the dual conviction that in the particular twists and turns, unique moments and continuous movements, ongoing developments and short-lived practices, lie: (1) invaluable resources of theological information, wisdom, and creativity for advancing the Church's mission and (2) fundamental belief in the times, places, and peoples of history—with all the ambiguity and conflict entailed—as the very medium of the Holy Spirit's work in the church and world. Put another way, this is to give priority to a sacramental model of church. As we saw above, Hellwig reads early Christian history as demonstrating a vitality of faith in the pastoral and communal aspects of the rituals and penitential practices that the bishop and many of the faithful shared in solidarity with those repenting of capital sins, as well as the turn to wisdom figures in the desserts and monasteries for supportive but also challenging counsel in ongoing conversion from sin in Christian life. Those historical witnesses, along with a charting of the mutually informing medieval evolutions of the priesthood and auricular confession, provide the resources for the concluding pastoral-theological proposals she proffers, sensitive to the majority of Catholics' alienation from the priest as judge and absolver in confession. In various prayer and support groups, communal penance services, personal companionship, and retreats, Hellwig recognizes the work of the same Holy Spirit evident in the range of practices in the first millennium. Common to all those practices is that they

> begin with an intensified experience of the loving and welcoming presence of God mediated by the warm, simple and unpretentious ministry of Christians to one another. This is what we mean by speaking of the Church as the body, or bodily presence, of the risen Christ . . . the basic sacrament of the presence and continuing action of God in Christ in the world.[75]

In contrast, the pope and bishops continue to operate out of an almost exclusively classical, Tridentine model, identifying the Church with the ordained hierarchy who teach, sanctify, and govern the laity by means of apodictic assertions only lightly considering history and, when doing so, rehearsing a history that carries out uninterruptedly the tenets of faith and morals provided in the timeless pages of Scripture. Thus, in his apostolic exhortation, *Reconciliation and Penance*, Pope John Paul acknowledges historical changes, but these are changes in a specific sacrament, which it is a "certainty that the Lord Jesus himself instituted and entrusted to the church" and that has always entailed confession of particular sins to an ordained minister.[76] In that type of ecclesiastical assertion lies the rub against both the careful historical-critical work of scholarly theologians and the popular dispositional tendencies of the vast majority of the Church's membership against such disciplinary instruction.

Sacramental theologians of recent decades, while certainly not questioning that forgiveness of sin is fundamental to the gospel of Jesus Christ and primordial to the mission of the church, nonetheless would question the pope's claims to the dominical specification that individuals make integral confessions of all serious sins to a priest for his judgment and absolution.[77] To cite but one further summary indicating how long a trajectory

---

75. Hellwig, *Sign*, 113–14.

76. John Paul II, *Reconciliation*, no. 30.

77. Limits of space and flow of argument prohibited me, above, from rehearsing Hellwig's historical survey of penance as including demonstration of the late-first-millennium dating for widespread practice of private confession to a priest, as well as how even as late as the early ninth-century court of Charlemagne, the role of the priest

was the development toward a theology and practice of auricular confession in the West:

> Patristic and early medieval discussion of ecclesiastical authority had concentrated on the possession by the episcopacy or papacy of the power of the keys. This had always, of course, involved the understanding that "the keys" pertained very specially to the church's ministry of forgiving sin; but a great deal of the discussion of the power of the keys had been directed to the persistent question of the relation between *sacerdotium* and *regnum*, i.e., to authority that was not specifically that concerned with the sacramental reconciliation of sinners. Such wider application of the notion of the keys continues into the medieval theologians and canonists, but there is a much greater development of theology about the nature of sacramental confession and forgiveness, and the church's authority in this sphere.[78]

In that summary, Bernard Cooke demonstrates a fairly cautious assessment of what can and cannot be asserted about ancient tradition, even as the intent of his historical scholarship was to substantiate theologically reasonable possibilities for change in Roman Catholic rites that nonetheless would be faithful to Scripture and tradition.

As for how the laity has come to react to the characteristics of style and content in the modern-era papal magisterium, John Paul's 1984 apostolic exhortation and subsequent letters concerning the sacrament of penance, troublingly, comprise an arguably textbook case of what American moral historian Michael Lacey, drawing on Bernard Lonergan's theory of classical versus historical consciousness, explains as ecclesiastical positivism:

> The excessive simplicity of the model encourages the notion that on matters of faith and morals, the papacy's traditional, apparently boundless teaching field, belief and behavior around the globe can be centrally programmed to radiate outward from Christ's Vicar in the Vatican, a view that has been called ecclesiastical positivism. It is simply a matter of ensuring that the conditions of formal authority have been met, citing the documents that validate this,

---

in assigning penance was to pray to God for the penitent's forgiveness, as opposed to declaring absolution in the name of God. Hellwig later summarizes how the formal theology of sacramental penance emerged in the twelfth century as one of the seven official sacraments, a process including precision of formula. Significantly, in the formula for penance the priest now declares absolution not from penalties but from sin itself. See Hellwig, *Sign*, 69–70.

78. Cooke, *Ministry*, 467–68.

recalling appropriate precedents, writing up the lessons one wants to convey in the customary Vatican idiom, and then promulgating them—sending them out and down the line.[79]

While the exercises of authority Lacey has in mind concern moral doctrine and canon law, his argument can likewise serve to analyze sacramental doctrine (which, of course, also relates to canon law), as the following paragraph from *Reconciliation and Penance* vividly demonstrates:

> It is opportune to reflect more deeply on the reasons which order the celebration of penance in one of the first two forms and permit the use of the third form. First of all, there is the reason of fidelity to the will of the Lord Jesus, transmitted by the doctrine of the church, and also the reason of obedience to the church's laws. The synod repeated in one of its propositions the unchanged teaching which the church has derived from the most ancient tradition, and it repeated the law with which she has codified the ancient penitential practice: The individual and integral confession of sins with individual absolution constitutes the only ordinary way in which the faithful who are conscious of serious sin are reconciled with God and with the church. From this confirmation of the church's teaching it is clear that every serious sin must always be stated, with its determining circumstances, in an individual confession.[80]

The form of the papal argument asserts legitimate authority yet, to follow Lacey's theory, at this juncture of history lacks "legitimate persuasiveness,"[81] the qualities of which have changed for the vast majority of younger and middle-aged Catholics and even a plurality of older Catholics.[82]

---

79. Lacey, "Prologue," 8.

80. John Paul II, *Reconciliation*, no. 33.

81. Lacey, "Prologue," 8.

82. See Tentler, "Souls," 310. For further discussions of the current widening rift between the hierarchy and the majority of American Catholics over the nature and limits of magisterial authority, see Taylor, "Magisterial Authority," 259–69; and D'Antonio et al., "American Catholics," 273–92. To cite but a couple of notable assertions the latter draw from their research data: "All indications from social research are that acceptance of the Catholic Church's moral authority has been diminishing since Vatican II. . . . More authority is claimed than is accepted. . . . In the case of the Catholic Church today, the claims to authority are found in the catechesis of the Catholic Church, the encyclical letters of the popes, and the writings and public statements of the bishops. . . . While Catholics [in the latter twentieth century] continued to maintain strong ties to family and church, they were also becoming more and more a part of American society, with its emphasis on personal autonomy." D'Antonio et al., "American Catholics," 274–75.

The decisive turning point in the laity's turn to the authority of their own experience was the 1960s, when the decades-long struggles among the hierarchy, lower clergy, and laity over the nature and function of conscience in moral decision-making reached their climax with the papal encyclical prohibiting artificial contraception within marriage. With growing numbers of Catholics already having come "to privilege . . . the lived reality of human relationships as a critical factor in moral deliberation," such that the stylized, truncated ritual of the confessional drifted away from individuals' exploration and formation of their consciences, *Humanae Vitae* catalyzed a complete break. Public conversation about the crisis, as advocated by moral theologian Richard McCormick to the US bishops in the early 1970s, did not fit the authoritative model to which the hierarchy was committed. Century's end fully realized McCormick's warning that their refusal would only exacerbate the laity's complete shift to considering the moral domain entirely their own, each individual reaching decisions with no consideration of the Church's teaching as binding or even relevant, especially in matters of sexual ethics.[83] With the latter historically having been prime serious matter for auricular confession,[84] Pope John Paul and the Vatican's strategy to renew the laity's fervor for regular confession could not but yield scant results. The use of ecclesiastical positivism to assert the authority of both the doctrinal teaching and disciplinary regulations and practices of the sacraments over a laity who largely either oppose or have become indifferent to this type of ecclesiastical power in relation to the contemporary complexities of social and personal life, ironically, if not tragically, assures the deterioration of the sort of communal, corporate life and mission, clergy and laity together, for a Church that all agree should be a living, salvific sign of reconciliation and conversion among its members and to the world.

Practice of Ministry and Sacrament: One Pastoral-Liturgical Proposal

That the present era is one of crisis for Roman Catholicism, fraught with a range of anxieties across the clerical and lay spectrum of the ecclesial body of the baptized, is exemplified in the writings on penance, sacramental liturgy, and (moral) authority by John Paul II, Monika Hellwig, and the social scientists and historians I have cited in this present study. In the face of the

83. See Tentler, "Souls," 310.
84. See Stotts, "Obedience," 97–99.

now decades-long rift between the hierarchy's and laity's perspectives on and (non-)practices of auricular confession, if not the seemingly impossible odds for a practical resolution, Pope John Paul did what any leader must by concluding his apostolic exhortation *Reconciliation and Penance* with an "Expression of Hope."[85] In times of such uncertainty and seemingly irresolvable differences, the members of a social body need such words from their leadership (however they might receive them). No small consolation for the Church's present generation rests in the fact that the apostolic author of the First Letter of Peter (see 1 Pet 3:15) needed to exhort the earliest church communities always to be prepared to give to anyone the reason for their hope. Indeed, that danger and division, fear and uncertainty (*ad intra* and *ad extra*), have accompanied the Church's mission continuously from the start makes hope in trials a veritable tradition of the faith.

Surely, the current crises of authority (that of the hierarchy, that in the sacramental-liturgical tradition, that of the laity) will not resolve themselves any time soon. In these early decades of the twenty-first century, Roman Catholicism functions in an age of epochal anthropological change—social, psychological, biological, and ecological. Put simply, how humans go about being human is rapidly evolving in the vortex of technologies, personal screen-oriented, mass-mediated culture, hyper-sexualized visualization and imagination, and all this hemmed in from many sides by the reason, if not laws, of the market economy. In such light, the issues of personalism and individual autonomy in matters of faith and morals for Roman Catholics of the latter part of the twentieth century might now seem almost quaint.

Add to this morphing anthropological mix the dissolution of socio-traditionally structured time, and one is not surprised by the deterioration of regular participation in Sunday liturgy, holy days of obligation, and biblically-traditionally shaped observances of the major seasons of the Church Year. And yet, even the younger generations of Roman Catholics value the Church's presence in society (whether locally or globally, the latter perhaps best attested by the media-sustained popularity of the modern papacy). They expect the Church to "be there" for them, and this not least in the availability of sacramental celebrations, for their personally constructed appropriation. In this regard, Lacey provides one further helpful observation:

> In terms of formal authority, there is in Catholicism no appeal beyond the pope. His word is the last word. In reality, however, those

85. John Paul II, *Reconciliation*, no. 35.

who practice a selective Catholicism, which includes nearly everyone, justify their choices, their refusal to follow to the letter all the instructions handed down from Rome, by appealing privately from a church that does not understand to a God who does. Their theism is intact, as are their sense of integrity and a spirituality of sorts. . . . Most laypeople appear willing to settle for simply keeping the rudiments of the sacramental life conveniently accessible, a hope now jeopardized by the priest shortage. Beyond that, they continue to deal with the rest of the instruction of conscience that comes down from above as best they can.[86]

As with John Paul's concluding expression of hope for his apostolic exhortation or the pastoral author of 1 Peter in his instruction on hope, here there is no need for cynicism. We should not delude ourselves about how committed to doctrine and polity the masses of laity were in any era of Christendom so as to be disappointed in the comparative present state of affairs. Highly significant is the fact that the rather tenuous link between the laity and hierarchical leadership in this evolving present era is the people's "keeping the rudiments of sacramental life." And so, I conclude with a practical proposal for exploiting one of the days on the liturgical calendar that remains popular for at least a strong plurality of Roman Catholics[87] as opportune for liturgical ministry to penitential conversion and reconciliation: Ash Wednesday.

Ash Wednesday is the symbolically charged moment in the Church Year that summons all the faithful, in whatever station of life, to embrace Lent as a gracious journey of conversion, whose destination is the renewed baptismal promises and refreshing waters celebrated at the Easter font. The requisite ritual commencing Lent includes not only the imposition of ashes—sacramental of our common humanity (mortality and its surrogate, sinfulness) before God the All Merciful—but also the proclamation of the biblical word eliciting an examination of conscience and mutual prayer of intercession. While the Roman Missal includes a proper Mass for Ash Wednesday, I would argue that what it presents as optional, namely, a liturgy of the word with blessing and distribution of ashes followed by prayers of intercession, a blessing and dismissal, better serves the purpose of the day in relation to the entire Easter cycle.

86. Lacey, "Prologue," 16.

87. According to relatively recent scientific polling data, 45 percent of US Catholics participate in the ritual observance of Ash Wednesday. See CARA, "Most Catholics."

Ash Wednesday is not a solemnity or feast obligating the faithful to participate at Mass. Indeed, the penitential character of the day finds many people present whose need for sacramental reconciliation with God, church, and self prohibits their participating fully in the Communion Rite (discipline Pope John Paul reiterated in his apostolic letters). But looking to the larger pastoral-ecclesial context, here is a stellar case for resisting the widespread post-Vatican II custom among American Catholic clergy of imposing the Mass as the sole communal rite signaling pastoral importance and ecclesial dignity. Making this case becomes increasingly urgent as the numbers of priests available for all these Masses continues its freefall as their increasingly elderly average age climbs ever higher.

Mass is not the optimal rite for Ash Wednesday; rather, the specific pastoral nature of the Lenten season logically points to the Rite of Penance and specifically to the model penitential celebrations provided in its Appendix II.[88] If Ash Wednesday is about calling the faithful to repentance and, moreover, if individual confession with absolution comprises the proper sacrament for those who have seriously sinned, then the liturgy for the day should devote the precious time available to helping the faithful discern their spirits in light of the gospel and by means of key traditional practices: communal song, preached word, examination of conscience, act of repentance (in this case, the reception of ashes), general intercessions, and dismissal exhorting all to mutual support, prayer, and individual penance (as needed and celebrated at some point in the forty days). That list, in fact, is a combination of the Missal's elements for Ash Wednesday's liturgy of the word and the Rite of Penance's sample penitential celebrations. In making this proposal, I consider myself to be building on the pastoral-theological wisdom Monika Hellwig gleaned from the strengths of the penitential ritual practices of the early Christian era in her advocacy for recognizing and advancing contemporary practices of reconciliation and conversion emerging among the faithful in the Church.[89]

The Rite of Penance outlines the "Benefit and Importance" of penitential services in terms explicitly resonant with the liturgical spirituality of Lent and perfectly suited to the communal celebration of Ash Wednesday:

> Penitential services are very helpful in promoting conversion of life and purification of heart.
>   It is desirable to arrange them especially for these purposes:

88. See "Rite of Penance," Appendix II, nos. 1–19.
89. Hellwig, *Sign*, 108–19. See also Kidder, *Making Confession*, 201–8.

—to foster the spirit of penance within the Christian community;

—to help the faithful to prepare for individual confession that can be made later at a convenient time;

—to help children gradually form their conscience about sin in human life and about freedom from sin through Christ;

—to help catechumens during their conversion.

Penitential services, moreover, are very useful in places where no priest is available to give sacramental absolution. They offer help in reaching that perfect contrition that comes from charity and that enables the faithful to receive God's grace through a desire for the sacrament of penance in the future.[90]

Appendix II outlines two sample "Penitential Celebrations During Lent," one emphasizing "penance as strengthening or restoring baptismal grace" and the other showing "penance as a preparation for a fuller sharing in the Easter mystery of Christ and his Church."[91] Adapted and combined with the proper readings and collects for Ash Wednesday and the imposition of ashes as the communal act of repentance, either version offers the structure and content for a pastorally beneficial liturgy for setting the people on their personal courses toward Easter.

The homily and general intercessions for Ash Wednesday are of irreducible importance for opening members of the faithful and the community as a whole to the impressive range of ways various individuals may find themselves celebrating the sacraments not only at the Easter Vigil, but also on the Sunday morning and throughout the entire Easter season. Immediately obvious are the catechumens being elected for baptism, confirmation, and Eucharist at the Easter Vigil, but other types of initiates variably populate Ash Wednesday's assemblies, as well: youngsters preparing to receive First Communion during the seven Sundays of Easter, teens preparing for the sacrament of confirmation to be celebrated at some point in the fifty days, parents and godparents looking forward to the baptism of infants on either Easter or subsequent Sundays, adults or older children entering into full communion in the church, and the seriously sick and elderly who would benefit from a celebration of the sacrament of anointing during Mass on one of the Sundays in the Easter Season. All of these the

90. "Rite of Penance," no. 37.
91. "Rite of Penance," Appendix II, no. 7.

Ash Wednesday preacher should exhort to participate as vigorously as possible in their respective meetings and activities, as well as the sacrament of penance, during the Lenten forty days so as to be optimally disposed to the graced events coming for them in Eastertide. The prayers of the faithful, to be announced after all have received their ashes, should include intercessions for all such specific groups.

Then there are the customary practices that still engage people's imaginations—and in many cases, actual commitments[92]—during the Lenten season. The Liturgy of the Word calls the community to prayer, fasting, and almsgiving, but these for the purpose of disposing the faithful toward, interceding for, and helping others to receive whatever graces the Spirit of the crucified and risen Christ may be offering to people in the current realities of their lives. All of this is not so much a matter of "giving up" things as a test of one's willpower or resolve, let alone of "making it up to Jesus" for what he has suffered for each of us personally. The extraordinary, prayerful, or penitential efforts made during Lent, rather, are a matter of conversion, of turning again to the Lord, of seeking in the depths of hearts and across the breadth of societies the face (see Ps 27:8) of the one who in the Church's rites reveals his paschal mystery as our own.

The promotion and fostering of such practices would meet the popular desire, which Hellwig had already identified among the faithful a few decades ago, for communally hearing the word of God concerning conversion together in liturgical assembly while leaving open personal deliberation and discernment about how to respond. This would frame the entire season of Lent as one of penitence, for which people would be invited to avail themselves of auricular confession if the matter upon which they find arising from the response to the Lenten lectionary leads them to the sacrament at some point in the forty days. No naïve panacea for the significant difficulties penance and pastoral-liturgical ministry face in the early twenty-first century, such practices nonetheless might promise one practical strategy true to tradition and, thus, to the needs of living Christians in a Church moving forward.

---

92. The 2008 poll found 60 percent of self-identified adult US Catholics abstain from meat on Lenten Fridays, 38 percent give up or abstain from something else during Lent, and 45 percent, besides giving something up, do something positive, including additional almsgiving for the needy. See CARA, "Most Catholics."

Part III

Liturgy and Ethics,
Scripture and Tradition

5

Baptism

Biblical Formation of Sacramental and Ethical Identity

Initiation into the Inevitable Question of Worship and Ethics: A Pastoral Tale

IT WAS A DARK and stormy night. Torrents of rain lashed the windows of the ample third-floor parlor in the parish house in Greenwich Village, New York City, where the RCIA group was in the midst of the two-hour Tuesday evening meeting that, along with the parish's principal Sunday liturgy, comprised their weekly practice from September through April, in the mid-1980s. At that point in early February the group's "journey" had reached the juncture pivoting on the Rite of Election, the church's calling each of the six candidates to full initiation in the Roman Catholic Church, to take place at Easter. Discerning the call with each candidate had been the RCIA director, Sister Anne, who, in her first year on the pastoral staff, had assembled eight parishioners as sponsors in the program, along with myself, a Jesuit scholastic in graduate studies. The total group, men and women ranging in age from mid-twenties to late sixties, had reached a certain level of familiarity with one another. Friendships had formed to the point of each candidate having a specific sponsor within the larger group. Affinities and dissonances among personalities, as one might expect, had also emerged, and these came to unprecedented expression with that night's agenda.

In view of the impending Rite of Election, Sister Anne invited the sponsors and candidates to share what full participation in the life of the Church meant to them. Strong differences of opinion among some of the sponsors, which apparently had been festering in their psyches for some time, exploded in an argument over whether the principal—or even the sole—reason for being a Roman Catholic was celebration of the sacred liturgy or, on the contrary, service to the poor and advocacy for social justice. As the content of the two positions became increasingly polarized the rhetoric reached heightened polemics. One of the men insisting on the exclusive priority of the Church's sacramental rituals came to invoke the story of Martha and Mary, from the Gospel of Luke. His recollection of the text bore certain embellishments, including his putting in Jesus' mouth an explicit identification of Mary's sitting at his feet with a life of prayer and worship as the singular mission of the Church in its members. A passionate opponent then enlisted her own memory of Luke's story, casting Martha as the paragon of Christian service to those in need—in this case the hungry, as personified by the Jesus who had come to her home for supper. The liturgical proponents howled, others looked perplexed by further interpretations people jumped in to offer, and still others were visibly worried by the display of raw, negative emotions escalating in the argument.

I scrambled to find a copy of the Bible and managed to get a word in edgewise. All agreed, with relief, to my offer to read the actual passage, which I did. The content of Luke 10:38–42 sounded surprisingly brief in the wake of the runaway debate. Jesus' concluding words, "Mary has chosen the better part," seemed to land unequivocally on the now silent room. The simplicity of the account bespoke the extent to which people had been presenting interpretations of the story as verbatim quotations from the text. I gently observed that such is not unusual and that, furthermore, the hermeneutical process is what keeps any story within a tradition alive: people have to share it, work with it. But that, I pointed out further, was what Luke himself had done in composing his Gospel. Primitive eucharistic communities had been hearing and passing on numerous stories of Jesus' words and deeds, some of which each of the four evangelists had eventually selected and placed in a particular order so as to write a compelling, convincing message about Jesus as Lord.

And so, I turned again to our short passage in question. I noted how the story immediately preceding it is the parable of the Good Samaritan (10:25–37), while the passage directly following Martha and Mary depicts a Jesus at prayer responding to his disciples' request, "Lord, teach us to pray" (11:1). Our enigmatic tale of Martha and Mary, it turned out, Luke had placed at the juncture of two chapters, linking what has become the most recognized parable about service to neighbor, the Good Samaritan, with the most readily recited Christian prayer, the Our Father (11:2–4). Might his having done so, I proposed, not give us a hint that divine worship in prayer and human care in service are not unrelated in the praxis of Christian faith, that the two are irreducible and indispensable, even if prayer is essential to grounding all life's activities?

Liturgy and Ethics in the Theological Academy: The Developing State of the Question

I begin this academic presentation on baptismal liturgy and ethics with this pastoral tale so as to articulate several cautions necessary when venturing into the dangerous territory of liturgy and ethics. That the topic appears dangerous is a good sign. For, as Johann Baptist Metz has taught us, situations fraught with danger rescue the content of the gospel from banality so that its import for decisions about life, human and Christian— especially when threatened in whatever context—can become a source of rescue itself. That the terrain for worship and ethics is indeed rough has been evident to liturgical and moral theologians now for more than a few decades. In the late 1970s, a Yale-based colloquy between Methodists Paul Ramsey, an ethicist, and Don Saliers, a liturgical theologian, and Catholic moral theologian Margaret Farley proved generative of sustained critical discussion.[1] Drawing upon the burgeoning sub-discipline of character ethics, Saliers claimed a conceptual and intrinsic, rather than merely external and causal, relationship between liturgy and ethics, arguing that prayer and worship over time form believers in deep affections characteristic of biblically inspired Christian tradition.

Saliers's argument resonated with concerns confronting liturgists and ethicists in their respective fields. In the rapidly changing modern environment, including the role of the churches and religious faith therein,

1. See Ramsey, "Liturgy," 139–71; Saliers, "Liturgy," 173–89; and Farley, "Beyond," 191–202.

liturgical theologians increasingly had to address the problem of liturgy's relevance. By tapping into the arguments of various moral and fundamental-critical theologies, certain liturgical theologians were able to produce apologetics against those who over-identify liturgy with ethics to the point of reducing the latter to the former. This leaves liturgical practice, in whatever inevitably flawed human context, wide open to charges of hypocrisy. On the other hand, across the whole range of Christian communities one can also hear voices insisting that liturgy has nothing to do with ethics, that the act of explicitly, communally worshiping God is the end in itself, and that any question of ethical import cannot but distort liturgy's rightful, singular purpose into an instrument for moral agendas.[2]

Among moral theologians during the same period was developing a contrasting concern to establish an explicitly, properly Christian ethics, as opposed to a practical do-gooder moralism, on the one hand, or a theoretical adoption of the philosophical lineage of Kantian autonomous reasoning, on the other—both of which marginalize the role of divine grace working through human community, agency, and action. Philippe Bordeyne has summarized the problem well:

> With hindsight it seems that [nineteenth- and twentieth-century moral theology's] search for harmony with modernity concluded by masking the very original contribution of Christianity to the moral formation of subjects, especially through catechetical, liturgical, and sacramental practices, or through charitable works.[3]

Bordeyne perceives a promising way forward—bridging Protestant and Catholic propensities to center virtues in the ethical quality of the community and the spiritual development of individuals, respectively—in William Spohn's argument for the sacraments as transforming encounters with the risen Christ, for liturgical participation as ongoing "growth in Christ's body that mobilizes faithfulness to the ethical call of Jesus."[4] Spohn reworks the fundamental question in the parable of the Good Samaritan in terms not of identifying one's neighbor but rather of discovering the believer's own identity: Who might I become if I follow Christ, if I go and do likewise? Bordeyne's own proposal for *identity-formation* as the nexus of liturgy and ethics, as we shall see below, aligns with performance theorists' arguments

2. See Westermeyer, "Liturgical Music," 193–95.

3. Bordeyne, "Ethical Horizon," 121.

4. Bordeyne, "Ethical Horizon," 125. See Spohn, *Go*, 87–99.

for the subjunctive character of ritual as the key to its function in the development and maintenance of human identity.

Meanwhile, back in the late 1990s, Saliers, in what has proven to be yet another generative, much-cited essay, addressed several substantial issues that had emerged from critiques of his earlier article on liturgy and ethics.[5] Predominant is the question of whether an abstract or purely conceptual notion of liturgy is adequate to the inquiry. Postmodern criticism rejects any appeal to liturgy in the abstract as bearing an unarticulated totalizing agenda about moral character, subject to a particular culturally induced interpretation of Christianity. Similarly, various liberationist theologies are suspicious of any conceptual claims about the ethically formative power of liturgy that fail to account for the operative power relations, and thus ethics, *within* the liturgy as practiced in a particular socio-historical and ecclesial context. While accepting these corrections, Saliers likewise insists that Christian liturgical traditions bear the disposition and means of self-critique. I would characterize this as the prophetic vein coursing through the living body of biblically based tradition and practice. Such criticism is directed to both Christians and their institutions—including their liturgical practices—and the wider culture in which they participate. The tension between normative liturgically based claims and ethical examination (both individual and corporate) is inherent to ritualization within any social body, a tension between the personally and socially cohering function of ritual and the probing desire for personal integrity and mutual accountability. That this is the case for Christian baptism is evident not only from my pastoral vignette above, but in the history of Christianity from the start.

A final and salutary caution from Saliers concerns the self-deluding error of any scholar attending exclusively to liturgical *texts* as if their content could convey what historically (either in the past or present) a given ritual might actually entail and affect among its participants—and even beyond them. Working with and through the resources of historical and social-scientific scholarship is obligatory when enlisting liturgical evidence from the past. Turning to the contemporary context, this drive beyond the text opens into consideration of "how mass media, social rituals [of sports events, the arts, entertainment, and the workplace], and 'lifestyle' options imaged in a consumerist society are far more powerfully formative of habit, perception, and moral character than are religious practices found

5. See Saliers, "Afterword," 209–24.

in Christian liturgy."[6] To this one can only respond, "Amen!" I would, none-theless, add the further observation that Christianity has always functioned symbolically and ritually in concert, and at times in conflicting tension, with a given host culture (noting, in the case of colonialism, the domination of the conquering culture), such that individual and communal Christian identity has been and continues to be forged in the matrix of a wider culture and a particular church as a subculture therein. Thus, clear-eyed recogni-tion of the extent to which contemporary Christian identity and practice is affected by the images and habits generated by our telecommunicating, consumerist, militarized, globalized, yet often nationalistic contexts is es-sential to avoiding any liturgical-textual positivism, that is, any notion that a rite such as baptism could singularly, unequivocally govern the thoughts, imaginations, and actions of any and every Christian participating in it. I say "Amen" to that.

Conversion-Initiation: Baptismal Symbols Constantly Reorienting Christian Lives

But I also say, with the sage Qoheleth: "There is nothing new under the sun" (Eccl 1:9b). For now, more than ever, historical, literary, anthropological, and archeological scholarship is helping us appreciate the extent to which the small and shaky venture of nascent Christianity was characterized by a search for communal and individual identity that had to be negotiated amidst the predominant social and cultural forces of the late-antique Medi-terranean world. The very content of the New Testament abounds with evidence that the first generations of Christians were people who needed a great deal of explanation and exhortation about who they were and what they were supposed to be about in their lives.[7] The Pauline and other apos-tolic letters, as well as the four Gospels, betray a range of ways in which the enigmatic belief in the crucified Jesus of Nazareth as risen Lord lent itself to notions of glory—an overly realized eschatology—or ambivalence or indif-ference toward society and neighbor and even fellow Christians that easily strayed down well-worn human paths of conventional virtue and vice or bounded off into uncharted territories of charismatic enthusiasm.

It is to those texts that became the New Testament that contempo-rary believers, such as that RCIA group in New York decades ago, turn

6. Saliers, "Afterword," 216.

7. See Lathrop, *Saving Images*, 53–70.

for authoritative answers at the origins of the faith. And yet, even as their memories and imaginations are amply impressed with outlines of such stories as Luke's Martha and Mary, the danger is always that their recall might be the pursuit of a pristine, primordial moment when all was clear, everyone sincere, the Christian content of faith and morals unadulterated by the messiness of psyches and bodies—natural and social. A fresh return to the normative narrative such as that of Martha and Mary, rather, models a life of faith in the company of the church that must always question, in the presence of Jesus, what life with him is all about. Once graced with the presence of the Lord Jesus at our house, what are we supposed to do?

"Brothers, what should we do?" (Act 2:37). In Luke's Acts of the Apostles, that is the people's response to Peter's proclamation of the executed Jesus as exalted Lord. The answer: get baptized. But that does not settle matters, does not finish the question about one's life in front of the disturbingly attractive message about Jesus. No, baptism does not settle things; rather, it *frames* them. By the time of Luke's writing, baptism, however varied in the details of its execution from place to place, functioned as a primary ritual and, thus, symbol of the Christian body, what social scientists John Seligman and associates call a "shared convention that indexes a shared world."[8] Indeed, the details in Peter's answer include the basic elements of baptism found across the New Testament: "Repent, and be baptized every one of you in the name of Jesus Christ so that your sins may be forgiven, and you will receive the gift of the Holy Spirit" (Acts 2:38). Receiving the gospel message, forgiveness of sin, invocation of Christ, immersion in water, infusion of the Holy Spirit—these comprise the complex of activities, variably realized in different contexts, that James D. G. Dunn has astutely argued the New Testament authors, reflecting conventional language of the earliest communities, render altogether as "baptism."

The word baptism functions as what Dunn calls a "concertina" term, comprehensively symbolizing the entire process of "conversion-initiation."[9] Dunn proposed the concept of "conversion-initiation" as a corrective to the mutually exclusive positions of twentieth-century New Testament scholars who, driven by their own theological ideologies, had been manipulating the textual details of the canonical corpus to prove that primordial Christianity was either a matter only of sincere personal

---

8. Seligman et al., *Ritual*, 105. Note: Hereafter, in the body of my text, I shall refer to the authors of this book simply as "Seligman."

9. See Dunn, *Baptism*, 5–8.

conversion, for which various ritual symbols were mere, even expendable expressions, or, alternatively, of submitting to the metaphysically effective ritual as the sole referent of the sacrament. Dunn's hyphenated joining of the two terms asserts that neither conversion nor initiation were (or now, are) expendable for Christians, that the ritual gestures that become the repertoire of symbols for Christian identity function, to employ Seligman's more recent terminology, in the subjunctive mode, creating and sustaining "an order that is self-consciously distinct from other possible social worlds."[10]

Returning one more time to the second chapter of Acts of the Apostles, we find Peter contrasting the call of Christ to the social order of the day, which he characterizes as "this corrupt generation" (Acts 2:40). The power in Luke's story at this point resides in the extent of its explicit articulation of the consequences of undergoing the ritual action of baptism, a reminder to Christian readers of how that by-then conventional Christian symbolic activity, which by nature of its physicality and repetition would function in ways open to or even at times devoid of any number of meanings, is meant to frame a sincere, that is to say reflexive, way of life. And, indeed, the passage concludes by describing a ritual pattern to which the first believers were devoted: "to the apostle's teaching and fellowship, to the breaking of the bread and prayers" (Acts 2:42). The description is elaborated in the chapter's remaining passage, describing sincere social and interpersonal ethical behavior (e.g., the sharing of possessions and goods in common) ritually framed with practices sustaining the moral character (and reputation) of the body: "Day by day, as they spent much time together in the temple, they broke bread at home and ate their food with glad and generous hearts, praising God and having the goodwill of all the people" (Acts 2:45–47a).

An alternate and probably more accurate rendering of the Greek, the NRSV translates as breaking bread "at home" would be "from house to house," better capturing the extent to which early Christianity took shape through social experimentation framed within the standard ritual patterns of the Hellenistic meal gathering. The evening meals' typical features of reclining several hours over food and drink partaken according to a set order and allowing for conversation, a ceremonial libation ushering in a symposium period of discourse and/or entertainment, and the presence of a variety of marginal personages served altogether to express and consolidate

10. Seligman et al., *Ritual*, 20.

the values of community (*koinonia*), equality and friendship (*isonomia* and *philia*), and grace/generosity/beauty (*charis*) expressed as utopian socio-political values.[11] These dynamics are what Seligman means by the subjunctive character of ritual, how ritual patterns create an experience *as if* the world were so. Repeated ritual enactment shapes or frames the identity of its participants so that, in this case, they become conditioned to act *like* a Christian.

The extent to which the meals, as well as the ritual enactment of baptismal symbols, affected the apostolic leaders' desired sincerity among the members and, thus, the genuineness of the community was, of course, always a mixed result, necessitating the ongoing dynamic tension of ritual and ethics (and, indeed, the ethical *in* ritual activity). Clearly, Luke presents at the outset of his Acts of the Apostles the ideal performance of Christian identity as a social body and in its members. The letters by and attributed to Paul, on the other hand, as well as the pastoral letters and even the Gospels, attest to the Christian communities' needs for explanation and exhortation to correlate their attitudes and daily behavior with the rituals they perform. Paul, laboring to explain to the Galatians their identities as members of the Christian community, turns to baptism and the imagery of taking on a new garment—Christ himself—to whom they now belong, making them all heirs of Abraham, regardless of ethnicity, free/slave status, or gender (Gal 3:27–28). He arrives at a similar (subjunctive) leveling of statuses by referring the Corinthians back to their baptism "in the one Spirit" to explain how they *should* consider themselves "one body" (1 Cor 12:13), respecting and exercising their various yet mutual gifts accordingly in service to the benefit of all. My point here (without any pretention to an exhaustive list or study) is that Paul enlists baptismal symbols to teach believers what their attitudes and actions should be like. Likewise, at the outset of 2 Corinthians, Paul asserts both his authority and sincerity by having the community recall with him their baptismal identity: "But it is God who establishes us with you in Christ and has anointed us, by putting his seal on us and giving us his Spirit in our hearts as a first installment" (2 Cor 1:21–22). That last explanation of the baptismal Spirit-gift, however, points to the ambiguous eschatological tension in which Paul (and the rest of the New Testament) perceive Christians—and indeed, the whole creation—to be living.

True to all human ritual, baptism negotiates ambiguity without completely resolving it, as would, in contrast, a discursive explanation. Indeed,

11. See Taussig, *In the Beginning*, 26–27.

the ambiguity that haunts all boundaries in life—physical, social, and traditional—is, as Seligman asserts, the very reason for ritualizing.[12] Ritual is the way we humans hold the many irresolvable ambivalences of life in a *both-and* tension that orients and, with repetition, reorients a person's identity and agency amidst the ambiguities of social relations and the individual life cycle—with death looming large over it all. Paul's most extensive commentary on baptism, Romans 6:1–14, bespeaks the ambiguous, permanent liminality (an oxymoron) into which a Christian is initiated for the duration of his or her earthly life.

What occasions Paul's treatment of baptism in Romans is his need to deal with the ambiguity in the Christian message as discussed in the letter's preceding chapter 5; namely, the seeming conclusion that if God meets humanity's increasing sinfulness with a greater abundance of grace in Christ, then Christians can "continue in sin in order that grace may abound" (Rom 6:1). In support of his emphatic denial of that view, Paul turns first to baptism:

> Do you not know that all of us who have been baptized into Christ Jesus were baptized into his death? Therefore we have been buried with him by baptism into death, so that, just as Christ was raised from the dead by the glory of the Father, so we too might walk in newness of life. For if we have been united with him in a death like his, we will certainly be united with him in a resurrection like his. (Rom 6:3–5)

On the basis of the inextricable connection between the one and the many—within the corporate or inclusive person of Christ[13]—Paul can say that we have died with Christ (see Rom 6:8a). Just as Christ's once-for-all death and resurrection was in history and yet also was eschatological, so the individual believer becomes part of the eschatological dominion of Christ by his or her decision to become subject to Christ in baptism.[14] The fundamental decision of dying to sin was made by Christ (Rom 6:10). The believer participates in the decision of that inclusive person she or he now claims as Lord.

The decision that has happened *to* humanity is the death and resurrection of Christ. The definitive character of that event as already past Paul indicates in Romans 6:4 by using the aorist tense of the verb—"we have

---

12. Seligman et al., *Ritual*, 41–47.

13. See Tannehill, *Dying*, 20–30.

14. See Bornkamm, *Early Christian Experience*, 75–76; and Tannehill, *Dying*, 73.

been buried with him"—in describing each believers' baptism as death in the completed past. Christ alone, however, has experienced the completeness of physical death and the totality of the resurrection. In verse 5, Paul places union with the resurrected Christ in the future tense. Dunn notes the striking fact that Paul does not link baptism with the idea of resurrection, even though the actual ritual would lend itself well to that.[15] Similarly, Gunther Bornkamm explains that the sense of verse 4 is not mystical initiation; rather, Paul is stressing the future character of the believer's resurrection as already present by conducting one's life as a person freed from sin.[16] Paul's use of the perfect tense in verse 5—"we have been united with him in a death like his"—indicates action continuing into the present. Paul has established a tension between the degrees to which one can identify with Christ's death and resurrection, and out of this tension arises Christian ethics and conduct, which Paul develops in the next three chapters of Romans. Baptism is the decisive event in a Christian's past that made it possible for him or her to "walk" (the subjunctive in verse 4), that is, to act morally under the inclusive lordship of Christ toward the future glory of the resurrection.

My point in this exegesis of Romans 6 is to highlight how even in bringing what Seligman would call the non-discursive, performative ritual practice of baptism into discursive explanation, even to the point of fixing the meaning of the water ritual as the indicative manifestation of one's union with Christ's death, Paul's understanding of baptism nonetheless frames a still-ambiguous existence for Christians. As Dunn states, "The whole of life for the believer is suspended between Christ's death and Christ's resurrection . . . The very dying of believers is a life-long process."[17] This liminal state of Christian life, one might add, John likewise depicts through the ambivalent, boundary-bending image of being reborn or born from above, "born of water and Spirit" (John 3:3, 5), the very things that later in John's narrative flow from Christ's side in death and from his breath in resurrection. The First Letter of John spells out the implications for those who have been born from above: To say one loves God while showing contempt for neighbor, whether in word or deed, is to walk (i.e., ethically act) blindly in darkness (see 1 John 4:11). We note, here again, that John's exhortation comes to those already baptized. Baptism frames Christian identity and

---

15. See Dunn, *Baptism*, 143.

16. See Bornkamm, *Early Christian Experience*, 74.

17. Dunn, *Romans*, 331.

action in the way, truth, and life of Christ, but this as a project fraught with ambiguous tensions—"No one has ever seen God, but if we love one another . . ." (1 John 4:12)—requiring constant recourse to word and sacrament. Likewise, in returning to Paul we learn that the "death" the new Christian experiences in baptism is the beginning of an ongoing process of "dying" that is the vocation of the Christian life. This "dying" is only salvific (life-giving) because it is inextricably linked with the resurrection which Christ, the source of life, himself alone now fully lives, yet shares with believers through his Spirit "as a first installment" (2 Cor 1:22). Ritually, communally shared knowledge of this future destiny assured in the risen Christ draws believers' lives forward on a course characterized by words and deeds, both ethical and ritual, revelatory of his redeeming power.

Christians need constant symbolic, ritual contact with both poles, the ethical and the ritual/symbolic, of this dialectic we liturgically identify as the paschal mystery. The regular, weekly way (from Scripture and earliest, continuous tradition) this happens is through celebration of the Eucharist. And so, we can note how Paul's method for correcting the Corinthians' ethically deficient parody of the Lord's Supper was by handing on the tradition that identified the bread and cup as a proclamation of the Lord's death until he comes (see 1 Cor 11:23, 26). Moreover, the Church Year also provides the annual experience for the entire community to participate in and reflect upon the ritual and symbols of baptism at Easter, especially if there are adults or children to be baptized at the Vigil, as well as to participate in occasions of baptism for infants whenever these might be held in the community. Still, the timing and consistency of these practices within and across churches and ecclesial communions in the contexts of late modernity pose distinctive challenges and opportunities for baptismal identity-formation today.

Conclusion

This (necessarily limited) survey of the biblical-traditional roots joining baptism, Christian identity, and ethical agency accords with the seminal insight of Alexander Schmemann that time is of the essence for understanding how liturgical rites are revelatory of the gospel's truth in human lives and history. In his foundational work, Schmemann argued persuasively for the "liturgy of time" proper to Christianity, as inherited from biblical and apocryphal Judaism, a cultic "sanctification of time" in contrast to other

religions' cultic and mythic sacralizations of nature and seasons.[18] The purpose of the church's liturgy is to make time "eschatologically transparent,"
that is, to manifest the unfolding of people's lives in cosmos and history in
the key of the "eighth day," in the light of the crucified and risen one whose
spirit now is working a new creation even amidst the groaning of this passing world. In his day, Schmemann sought to correct what he described (and
despised) as the long-mistaken piety whereby Christianity came to understand Sunday on a par with all the other days of the week, functioning as
the complementary sacred break from the profane workaday schedule, a
matter of stepping into church to say prayers before heaven and then stepping back out into this world's mores of commerce, entertainment, and
self-realization.

Our pastoral-theological challenge today, however, as Philippe
Bordeyne has pointed out, is the social de-structuring of time causing
self-alienation in (increasingly globalized) lives devoid of the rhythms of
ritual and periods of meditative reflection.[19] Bordeyne argues for exploiting Christians' increasingly episodic approaches to liturgical participation
in the "powerful moments" of life-passage rites and major calendrical feasts
as the key to identity-formation. That pastoral agenda finds confirmation
in practical theologian Charles Foster's theory of event-based education.
Acknowledging that Christian traditions of daily and weekly worship
practices are too weak to reverse the tide of the 24/7 timeless cycling and
individual tailoring of time, Foster argues for how believers can nonetheless grow in faith through occasion-based events of worship wherein the
interplay of cognitive and affective engagement generate meaning, identity,
and purpose in the lives of the participants.[20] The ongoing challenge, then,
is to develop robust pastoral-liturgical practices of baptism for infants and
adults. By whatever combination of seasonal and episodic occasions, the
goal is to afford original opportunities for Christian identity-formation
amidst and in service to the undeniably ambiguous vicissitudes endemic to
human living and, indeed, to the gospel itself as God's kenotic immersion
therein.

18. See Schmemann, *Introduction*, 69–80.
19. See Bordeyne and Morrill, "Baptism," 164–74.
20. See Foster, *Educating Congregations*, 12, 49, 68, 89.

6

Participation in Mystery

Liturgical-Ethical Inquiry into Tradition

Introduction

THIS ESSAY'S TASK IS to pursue the persistently evasive articulation of the relationship between Christian liturgy and the ethical and political lives of Christians in the world. Several decades have passed since such paragons of political and liberation theologies as Johann Baptist Metz, Gustavo Gutiér-rez, Dorothee Sölle, and Edward Schillebeeckx insisted that Christian faith is first and foremost praxis, a praxis of mysticism and politics, of liturgy and ethics. Some among the subsequent generations of theologians, myself included, have sought to capitalize on that fundamental insight, genera-tive yet seemingly incomplete or, perhaps better understood, inexhaust-ible—inexhaustible because concerned with unfathomable divine mystery being revealed in the limited, ever-passing personal, interpersonal, and social corporeality of human existence. To ponder the connection between liturgy and life is to pose a question that, moreover, from the perspective of bodily human subjectivity, people really do not want to entertain, and not because of bad character but because of an unarticulated, fundamental sense of the nature of human ritualizing. Put simply, we humans ritualize because of the ambiguities in life.[1] Things that we can explain, discuss,

---

1. Notable treatments of this aspect of the human phenomenon of ritualizing include Bell, *Ritual Theory*, 92, 108–17; and Seligman et al., *Ritual*, 17–67.

argue about, well, we explain and discuss and argue about them. We ritualize when dealing with matters more ambiguous, defying discourse and
explanation. Thus, to pursue articulation of the *meaning* of what we do in
sacramental rites and what that *means* in relation to ethical behavior and
socio-political engagement is to go against the grain of our human fabric.
And yet, the practical nature of the divinely revealed content of Christian
faith compels the foolhardy human endeavor.[2] I overcome my trepidation
here by the repairing to the fundamentals of liturgy, in terms of human
participation in divine mystery, so as to see if such ressourcement might
refresh intellectual theological insight or, even better, make some small
contribution to invigorating practice, liturgical and ethical.

The Necessity of Liturgy for Christian Faith[3]

An adequate understanding of Christian liturgy, as part of the broader activity of divine worship, fundamentally depends on recognizing what God
it entails. The content, shape, and scope of Christian worship is a function
of the God who is both its subject and object, namely, the God of biblical
revelation, the God of Jesus, the triune God revealed through his life, death,
and resurrection.[4] This apparently innocent, if not seemingly tautological,
statement is a stick of theological dynamite that, when ignited by the gift of
faith in the gospel, explodes conventional notions of divine worship, breaking down the barriers narrowly confining it to cultic activity, that is, to
religious ritual. Put simply, worship of God is the entire Christian life, and
thus the entire mission of the church in the world. Liturgy is the symbolic,
ritual activity of the assembled church. It gives believers an explicit sense,
a tangible manifestation, of the God hidden in their daily lives, as well as
something of the specific content, through proclaiming and responding to
Sacred Scripture, of what this ongoing human encounter with the divine
is like.[5] In the church's liturgy, believers glorify God by participating more

2. For one highly original attempt at reconciling the biblically based yet ritually realized qualities of Christian liturgy, see Mitchell, *Meeting Mystery*, 3–146.

3. The content of the following three sections is taken directly, with some additions
and minor changes, from Morrill, *Divine Worship*, 5–11. The author thanks Liturgical
Press for permission to use this copyrighted material.

4. See Chauvet, *Sacraments*, 155–61.

5. For a discussion of the necessity of the content of biblical proclamation, as well
as its event-quality in dialectical relation to manifestation—the dynamic of word and
sacrament—for the practice and understanding of Christianity, see Tracy, *Analogical
Imagination*, 217–18.

deeply in God's vision for the world, and their place in it, through word and sacrament.

Thus, Christians have an irreducible need for the liturgy, the *ritual* worship, they celebrate, even as those sacramental rites do not in themselves comprise the total practice of the faith, the single locus for knowing the one true God and his Son, Jesus Christ. The Second Vatican Council's Constitution on the Sacred Liturgy articulates this dynamic of Christian ecclesial life by stating, "the liturgy is the summit toward which the activity of the Church is directed; at the same time it is the font from which all her power flows."[6] To speak in terms of source and summit indicates that liturgy, while unequalled in its efficacious realization of the Church as Christ' body in union with him as head,[7] nonetheless is not the sole work of the Church and its members. Liturgical rites, rather, guide and nourish all the activity of believers' lives, creating the possibility of encountering God therein. Christian faith is a praxis in the world.[8] Guided by the ever-beckoning summit revealed in the Church's sacramental worship, believers traverse a worldly terrain experienced as the *creation* in which God delights in granting them active roles and, moreover, gives them the living water (John 4:14), the bread of life (John 6:35), to sustain them in this co-creative, salvific process. To join in Holy Wisdom's ongoing work in the history of suffering and the promise of ultimate triumph for all her creatures *is* to worship God.[9]

Over the past century-and-a-half, theological scholarship and official church leadership have adopted the term "liturgy," based on the ancient Greek concept *leitourgia*, meaning public work done from among and for the benefit of a people, to recover the proper, fundamental sense of worship found in Scripture and most ancient tradition.[10] In contrast to such terminology as (the American) going to or (German) hearing or (Irish) getting one's Mass or (the French) assisting at divine offices or (near-universal) receiving a sacrament, the rhetoric of liturgy revitalizes the ancient sense of the Church's sacramental rites as the symbolic and, in the power of the Holy

---

6. Paul VI, *Sacrosanctum Concilium*, no. 10.

7. See Paul VI, *Sacrosanctum Concilium*, no. 7.

8. See Metz, *Faith in History*, 84, 154–55. See also Gutiérrez, *Essential Writings*, 31–32, 57, 267.

9. See Johnson, *She Who Is*, pt. III; and Crainshaw, *Wise*, 149–58.

10. See Dalmais et al., *Principles*, 7–9, 229–34.

Spirit, very real participation of all the faithful in the divine-human *mystery* of creation and redemption.

The Mystery of Faith: God's Glory in Humanity's Salvation

At the origins of Christianity, mystery is not about esoteric cults or secret rituals but, rather, the revelation that in the person and mission of the Jewish eschatological prophet Jesus of Nazareth, crucified by sin but raised to life by the Spirit, God's purpose for creation has been fulfilled. In Jesus, whom faith acclaims the Christ, God's boundless and merciful love for the suffering and the guilty *in the very context of human lives in history* has been definitively manifested. The mystery of Jesus' death and resurrection reveals that his words and actions, his total person and personal history, gave glory to God by saving and sanctifying people. In the Gospel of Luke, heavenly messengers proclaim at its outset the meaning of the entire life of Jesus that will follow: "Glory to God in the highest, and on earth peace to those on whom his favor rests" (Luke 2:14).[11] As the Christian tradition developed over the next few centuries, this inseparable relationship of divine glorification and human salvation (often termed "sanctification") would pervade the sermons, catechetical instructions, and letters of the Fathers of the Church. By the close of the twentieth century, the theologically and pastorally revitalizing potential of this recovery of ancient tradition became evident in the widespread quoting and paraphrasing of the words by Irenaeus of Lyons: "'For the glory of God is a living man, and the life of man consists in beholding God,' in the Spirit and through the Son, who is 'the visible of the Father.'"[12]

It is in this broader soteriological perspective that the meaning and purpose of Christian worship resides. The significance of the Church's liturgical form of worship does not lie in its cultic personages, objects, actions, and locations in themselves but, rather, in their symbolic function in relation to the biblical narratives which have revealed the entire cosmos and human history as the arena of God's creative and redemptive activity. What Christian liturgy is about is entirely a function of the specific God it worships—not the distant, mechanistic God of modern deism, nor the idealistic Transcendent in our personal experiences and feelings, nor the divine One "up there" who only appears in certain sacred places "down

11. See Minear, *To Heal*, 50.

12. Irenaeus, *Against Heresies* 4.20.7, quoted in Farrow, *Ascension*, 66.

here," but the God who covenants, that is, the God who has committed himself in love to the deliverance of humanity in history. This covenantal origin and basis of biblical faith is the reason worship is not a unidirectional ritual action done by believers for God but, rather a full-life response to the gracious love (*hesed*) and trustworthy faithfulness (*'emet*) God has shown the people,[13] compelling them to behave in kind:

> Hear, O Israel; our God is one Lord; and you shall love the Lord your God with all your heart, and with all your soul, and with all your might. (Deut 6:4–5; see also Matt 22:37)

> This is the great and first commandment. And a second is like it. You shall love your neighbor as yourself. (Matt 22:38–39; see also Lev 19:18)

The Christian church reads the Jewish biblical texts, the First (or Old) Testament, as a covenant history, focused on the climactic events of the Exodus and Mount Sinai, but founded in the promises to Abraham and the patriarchs and revitalized in the symbolic words and deeds of Isaiah, Jeremiah, and the other prophets. God chose Israel to be the recipients of this covenantal heritage, receiving through it the mission to be light to the nations (see Isa 42:6; 49:3, 6). The content of the covenant and the character of the God it reveals comprise the reason that sacred feasts and sacrifices are only pleasing if offered by a people actively striving for justice, mercy, and peace (see Amos 5:21–24; Mic 6:6–8).[14] The need for such justice and peace, nonetheless, points to their absence and, thus, to the evil and suffering with which human history is riddled in the presence of the all-powerful and all-loving, but thereby totally Other, God.

The Paschal Mystery: Covenantal Life in Christ Jesus

The testament of the first believers in Jesus as the Christ is that God's covenantal promise of deliverance to Israel was taken up and transformed in the person, mission, and message of Jesus, with his death and resurrection constituting the climactic moment of covenant history. The Gospels present Jesus as an eschatological prophet who claimed that Israel's longed for, final deliverance from exile, the reign of God, was coming about through

---

13. See Schillebeeckx, *Christ*, 82–89 [93–100].

14. For discussion of these texts, see Holmgren, "Priests," 304–16.

his words and actions.[15] The entire New Testament witnesses to the unexpected shape that God's faithfulness to Jesus took, raising him bodily from death into a new form of life, revealing his singular divine origin and end as the firstborn of a new creation that will one day be realized for all. This is the mystery revealed at the heart of Christian faith, the revelation that the strength of death is past and the promised covenant of love written on human hearts is underway. Jesus enacted this greatest of his parabolic actions[16] at the most important point in the Jewish cycle of sacrificial worship, the Passover, the memorial of deliverance from slavery and oppression that bore the promise that God would yet redeem his people definitively. In his mission and death, Jesus took on both the nation's plight and the form their obedience to the covenant needed to take. In raising the dead Jesus to life, God revealed a new, unexpected outcome for his Passover, the first installment of the resurrection of all humanity.

The mystery of Christian faith, then, is paschal, that is, pertaining to Passover and, more specifically, to Jesus himself as the definitive sacrifice.[17] The specific content of this paschal mystery needs repeatedly to be expounded, through word and sacrament, lest we lose sight of what God we are worshiping: the God who is for humanity, for the happiness and peace of all people, the God who is known in those who join in that activity, the God whose image is not sought in static objects but in actions. Liturgical theology, then, seeks to comprehend the vision and practice of Christian faith not in religious terms of sacred versus profane, but, rather, of mystery disclosed in history: "In doing [the liturgy], the Church pursues its most essential purpose, which is to ensure the active presence of divine realities under the conditions of our present life—and that is what 'mystery' means."[18] The paschal mystery likewise bears the pain of that which it does not disclose, the inexplicable wisdom in God's still waiting to deliver all the suffering into "a new heavens and a new earth" (2 Pet 3:13; Rev 21:1).[19]

15. My thought here has been greatly shaped by N. T. Wright's series, Christian Origins and the Question of God 2 and 3: *Jesus* and *Resurrection*, respectively.

16. See Minear, *To Heal*, 24.

17. See Daly, "Sacrifice Unveiled," 24–42.

18. Dalmais, *Principles*, 266.

19. In contrast to what he describes as Christian theology's long trivialization of suffering as an eschatological question, along with its pursuit of "too many clever answers to such questions as Who is God? And Where is God?" Johann Baptist Metz argues compellingly for a turn "to the primordial biblical question, What is God waiting for?" Metz, *Passion*, 58; see also 84.

In Jesus the categories of sacred and profane break down. Christian liturgy is not a matter of taking believers out of the world for a moment but, rather, of immersing them more deeply in the mystery of God's paradoxical purpose for it over time.[20] Sin is not what happens in the profane world, while sanctification can be found in some exclusively sacred, separate precinct. Rather than the religious division of sacred and profane, the categories shaping Christianity are past, present, and future.[21] The mutually informing ritual activity of word and sacrament draws those present in the Church's liturgical assembly into the memory of God's actions and promises of human redemption, transforming them, through the power of the Holy Spirit, into a foretaste of their promised fulfillment, when God will be all in all (see 1 Cor 15:28). Christians live in an utterly paradoxical time between the definitive inauguration of God's reign in the person of Jesus and the final realization of the whole creation's peaceful, just, and loving existence in God's presence. The two primary sacramental rites of the Church, baptism and Eucharist, reveal this paradoxical divine worldview, initiating and sustaining believers' participation or communion—their *koinonia*—therein. The Church celebrates the paschal mystery of Christ liturgically so that this mystery might be writ large across its members' lives in the world, embracing the "joys and the hopes, the griefs and the anxieties of the men of this age, especially of those who are poor or in any way afflicted."[22]

Participation/Koinonia:
Ancient, Fundamental Christian Principle

In the eleventh encyclical of his long papacy, John Paul II argued that the Church's ethical concern for threatened human life—across such issues as abortion, the arms trade, euthanasia and assisted suicide, care for the elderly and sick, capital punishment, human-reproductive technologies, drug abuse, unjust distribution of the world's resources, and the international

20. See Gutiérrez, *Power*, 31–33.

21. See Schmemann, 70–81, 183–84; and Morrill, *Anamnesis*, 87–115.

22. Paul VI, *Gaudium et Spes*, no. 1. Building on Paul's proclamation of a new social order in Galatians 3:28 and the gospel's eschatological vision of the reign of God, Bernard Cooke argues: "Such a global sharing of the Spirit of God will not be a specifically religious phenomenon but something as broad as human life worldwide. If and when it occurs, it will make clear that Christianity was not meant to be a religion in any narrow sense of the word but rather the catalyst for a whole new way of being human." Cooke, *Power*, 27.

arms trade—finds its basis in "the core of this Gospel . . . the proclamation of a living God who is close to us, who calls us to profound communion with himself and awakens in us the certain hope of eternal life . . . the affirmation of the inseparable connection between the person, his life and his bodiliness."[23] The fundamental evangelical category of communion (*koinonia*), the pope rightly highlights, is not a private or merely personal sharing of life between God and the individual but essentially a social phenomenon, as well. Citing the first letter of John's opening proclamation of believers' fellowship (*koinonia*) with the Father and Son as compelling their welcome of others into their fellowship (*koinonian*) with one another (1 John 1:3), the pope draws the implication: "We need to bring the Gospel of life to the heart of every man and woman and to make it penetrate every part of society."[24] In the course of developing his case for why the faithful should recognize the social-ethical human dimension of sharing (participating)—through word and sacrament—in the very divine life of Father, Son, and Spirit, John Paul draws on the patristic authors Irenaeus, Athanasius, and Gregory of Nyssa.[25]

The Church—as the assembly of a people for mission—stands to lose much if we neglect the primordial concept of participation, so prevalent in Scripture (across the entire range of epistles) and tradition (constant in the writings of Fathers around the entire Mediterranean). Indeed, I would propose that the notion of participation (fellowship, communion, sharing, partaking—all apt translations of *koinonia*) can prove helpful in the now decades-long quest among theologians—liturgical and systematic—to argue for an intrinsic relationship between sacramental worship and sociopolitical ethics.[26] Neglect, abandonment, or at least hesitation toward the concept might stem from a deeply rooted distrust of archaic Greek or, perhaps, later Scholastic metaphysical models—whether Platonic, Stoic, or Aristotelian—as having aided and abetted mystifying, dualistic patterns in Christian sacramental anthropology, both theoretical and practical. But I am wagering that a generous hermeneutical revisiting of the patristic notion of participation is promising, on the condition that we remember how the ancient Christian pastors were invoking common philosophical

---

23. John Paul II, *Evangelium Vitae*, no. 81.

24. John Paul II, *Evangelium Vitae*, no. 80.

25. See John Paul II, *Evangelium Vitae*, nos. 38, 80, 87.

26. Morrill, *Anamnesis*, 57–62; Gutiérrez, *Essential Writings*, 247–254; Schillebeeckx, *Christ*, 40–47 [55–61]; and Schillebeeckx, *Church*, 29–33 [30–33].

terminology and concepts to advance the practical life of the gospel, and not the other way around. Limited here to a brief overview, I shall focus on the work of Athanasius of Alexandria as representative of how participation functions in the literature of the first five centuries.

The notion of participation is part of what one could call the "philosophy" of early Christians, provided one understands from the start that philosophy in that era was a pursuit of knowledge as an entire way of life. For Christians, the end or purpose of such knowledge was a life of love, a practice, in the terminology of the fathers, of *virtues* and *piety* in the midst of a world struggling in the evil shadow of death, whose forces were immanent not only in the mutable and corruptible nature of each human person-body, but also in such threats to life in the social body as starvation, restrictive marriages, the dangers of childbirth, captivity and slavery, and various forms of illness.[27] The cosmic and social locations of the body in Christian antiquity lent themselves to the Fathers conceiving of the human condition in terms of dominion, of individuals participating within hierarchical social bodies under some power-figure's reign. Echoing Paul's soteriological anthropology in Romans 5 through 8, the patristic writers often described the forces of death in terms of the first Adam (swayed by the devil), an inclusive or corporate figure whose headship establishes the circumstances of every member of the human race. Deliverance comes through baptism and life in the dominion of Christ by the power of the Spirit.[28] People participate in one dominion or the other by the exercise of their own will. For Christians, the virtuous exercise of the (always mutable) will, as well as the assurance of victory over mortality, finds its source and sustenance in the celebration of the sacraments.

In his treatise *On the Incarnation of the Word*, Athanasius lays out an anthropology wherein humans, having been given a share in the very power of God's own Word, are created to enjoy reflecting the divine life through participation in such knowledge and to escape death's corruption by the grace of participating in the Word through the good exercise of their will.[29] Created out of nothing, and thus naturally bound to corrupt (or decay) and vanish, humanity was the object of God's special favor (grace) in giving

27. See Brown, *Body*, 5–17, 26, 218.

28. For treatment of that Pauline theology, see ch. 5 above. For an insightful contemporary description and analysis of force and fear as the historically basic paradigm of human power in and between societies, see Cooke, *Power*, 13–44.

29. Athanasius, "On the Incarnation," no. 3.3, 37.

knowledge, a "partaking of the Word," enabling humans to "live henceforth as God."[30] Such rationality entails exercise of the will, which, tragically, humanity in Adam practiced badly. Humanity's original participation in the image and likeness of God, through the Word, sustains God's special favor toward them, moving further God's pity for not only their natural corruptibility but also their outright subjection to death as their sovereign. Put another way, humanity lives under a continuous threat to the goodness of the life they have to share and, ultimately, the threat to life itself.

Out of love for his own, Christ the incarnate Word accomplished two works on humanity's behalf:[31] first (or of primary importance), his bodily death at the willful hands of humanity as death's defeat, with his bodily resurrection "a proof of the resurrection in store for all";[32] and second, his making himself, invisible as God the Father, manifest in his works as the very Word of the Father. By the latter, Athanasius has in mind Christ's mission as a teacher and healer, whereby he reorients humanity's vision to see how God (the true sovereign) really is at work among humanity. Believers now participate in that redeemed life, with the visible evidence for Christ's sovereign power witnessed in the humanly persuasive character exhibited by the martyrs, the continence of virgins and young men,[33] and as Athanasius recounts in his *Life of Antony*, the monks' exercise of their wills according to humanity's restored, original capacity to participate in divine life. Indeed, Athanasius has Antony describe Christ the Lord as their coworker in such good living[34]—a comment pointing toward the Spirit's empowerment through the sacraments. But first, I must pause to make my own comment.

Despite whatever degree of alienation we late-moderns might experience in such a heavily mythological and hagiographic delivery of the Christian message, we might nonetheless hear in Athanasius's writings a dynamic passion for the generous, life-giving love God, in Christ, exercises not only for but also among and through humanity. The exercise of our human wills is public, shared in social life, evidenced in bodies placed on the line and for the good of the entire human race, and not only the social

30. Athanasius, "On the Incarnation," no. 3.4–5, 38.

31. Athanasius, "On the Incarnation," no. 16.5, 45.

32. Athanasius, "On the Incarnation," no. 22.3, 48.

33. Athanasius, "On the Incarnation," no. 48.1, 62.

34. Athanasius, "Life of Antony," no. 19, 201.

body but, at least by the persuasion of witness through one's own bodies, the body politic.

How to conceive of such divine power in human corporality? Athanasius, in a move again paradigmatic of patristic soteriology, describes this in terms of deification. When Athanasius famously states toward the conclusion of his treatise on the incarnation of the Word, "For he was made [human] that we might be made God,"[35] the shape such deification (participation in God's Word) takes is in practice of the virtues. Moving from the conclusion of that text to the account of Antony, we find Athanasius likewise describing how the saint healed the suffering and afflicted "not by commanding, but by prayer and speaking the name of Christ. . . . Antony's part was prayer and discipline."[36] To speak of participation in the divine life, of deification, then, is not to claim for humans the very nature of God, is not to claim that humans become gods (although cultures to our present day exhibit the tendency of their members to bestow on their own godlike status). No, this patristic notion of deification entails the revelation of what God is doing precisely in the humanity of humans. In his *Third Discourse Against the Arians*, Athanasius writes: "For we all, partaking of the Same [Word], become one body, having the one Lord in ourselves. . . . [Christ] signifies those who become distantly as He is in the Father; distantly not in place but in nature . . ."[37] The distance is bridged, as it were, by the gracious gift of the Holy Spirit who, Athanasius explains in terms resonant with the Johannine tradition (see 1 John 3:24; 4:13), enables the Son to be "in" believers, and believers "in" him: "reasonably are we, as having the Spirit, considered to be in God, and this is God in us. . . . [By] the participation of the Spirit we are knit into the Godhead."[38] The Spirit, sharing in the same nature as God the Father and the Son, is able to divinize believers.

Baptism establishes one's participation in the divine life, endowing believers with the Spirit of God and, thereby, the grace for living the virtues. The Christian thus receives the means to strive against the mutability of the passions, against inconsistent practices of reason and will that hinder realization of a good way of life. The other evil from which Christ has saved humanity is corruption, that is, mortality. Participation in the sacrament of the Eucharist is the Christian's assurance that he or she is subject to

35. Athanasius, "On the Incarnation," no. 54.3, 62.

36. Athanasius, "Life of Antony," no. 84, 218.

37. Athanasius, "Third Discourse," no. 22, 406.

38. Athanasius, "Third Discourse," no. 25, 406–07.

neither death's dominion nor its ultimate claim but, rather, will be raised to immortality. Patristic literature is replete with this theme of immortality and immutability. With death comprising the dominion characterized by mutability of mind (the struggle to practice the virtues) and body (the uncontrollable changes wrought by both external—environmental, societal, interpersonal—causes and intrinsic—somatic—development and decline), the promise of immortality in Christ's dominion likewise reveals the power of the Spirit who raised him out of death so as now to be at work in the baptized—in body, mind, and spirit. A subsequent bishop in the Alexandrian line, Cyril, taught of the sanctifying power of the Eucharist—the life-giving flesh of the divine Word, the risen and ascended Christ—as communicants' participation in the life that abolished death's final threat to them.[39] Yet further to the east, in the decades between Athanasius and Cyril, was a pastor whose catechesis included a veritable tour de force—joining immortality and immutability, Spirit and body, Christ and Church, members and community, heaven and earth, sacrament and ethics—in his mystagogy of the Eucharist.

Theodore, bishop of Mopsuestia (d. 428), but while still a presbyter in Antioch, produced fifteen catechetical homilies that include two each on baptism and Eucharist.[40] In teaching on the latter, he explains that baptism has made the neophytes members of "a single body." Now, by the Spirit's grace in the eucharistic Communion, "they are to be firmly established in the one body by sharing the body of our Lord, and form a single unity in harmony, peace and good works."[41] Theodore's mystagogy of the words of invitation to Communion, "What is holy for the holy," expounds the intrinsic link between the sanctity of divine-human participation in sacrament with the recipients' will to live accordingly: "For our Lord's body and blood,

39. "So we approach the mystical gifts and are sanctified, becoming partakers of the holy flesh and the honorable blood of Christ the Saviour of us all. . . . For being by nature, as God, life, when he had become one with his own flesh, he made it life-giving." Cyril, "Third Letter," 352.

40 For a lengthier treatment of Theodore's sacramental theology and pneumatology, from which the present rehearsal is drawn, see Morrill, "Many Bodies," 24–33.

41. Theodore of Mopsuestia, "Baptismal Homily," 234. Augustine of Hippo, more famously, "gives an ecclesiological twist to the notion of our being changed into Christ's body through the eucharist, declaring the effect of eating the (eucharistic) body of Christ is that we are turned into the (ecclesial) body of Christ: 'For its effect . . . is unity, that having been made his body and having been made members of him, we may be what we receive (*simus quod accipiumus*)' (*Serm.* 57, 7, PL 38, 389)." Wainwright, *Eucharist and Eschatology*, 114.

which are our food, are indeed holy and immortal and full of holiness, since the Holy Spirit has come down upon them."[42] The Spirit's work is to sanctify Christ's body and blood, which is to say, to make them immortal. The medium of Christ's body and blood in this present age is sacramental, with the fully sanctified symbols of bread and wine conferring this holiness, this grace of sanctification, upon those who have been baptized. The life of holiness, however, is not a passive one for Christians: "You must lead good lives so as to strengthen in your own persons the gift which has been given you and to be worthy of the food you require."[43] Since the exercise of one's will is bound up with one's salvation, Theodore can explain how the Eucharist "feeds the soul as well as the body, and even more than the body."[44] The Christian's body and soul are destined for heaven, where Christ's body and soul already are. Strengthened by the "Lord's body and blood and the grace of the Holy Spirit," Christians "must all order our lives with a view to the world to come."[45]

Participation as Sanctification, Sanctification as Salvation

Given the central role of the Eucharist in the tradition of the Church, as the source and summit of its life in its members (so affirmed at Vatican II), my rehearsal of the ancient Christian notion of participation not surprisingly reaches its climax with the sacrament of Communion. The conclusion to my brief patristic itinerary finds an identification of participation with sanctification, with the latter having to do not with some isolated, sacred status but, rather, a divinely inspired and humanly willed practice of living in this world. Participation in the Eucharist is a partaking in the very holiness of God, a holiness embodied in the person of Christ, whose Spirit sanctifies participants' bodies with graces characteristic of how Jesus executed the will of his Father. Sharing in the vision of that reign through liturgy of word and sacrament, through the biblically charged symbolism of communion in true (life-sharing) food and true drink, the body and blood of Christ, believers are nourished in their desires to practice ethical virtues as realizations of God's will on earth, as in heaven. Still, such a summary, from classical Christian literature, of participation in sacramental mystery

42. Theodore, "Baptismal Homily," 238.

43. Theodore, "Baptismal Homily," 238.

44. Theodore, "Baptismal Homily," 243.

45. Theodore, "Baptismal Homily," 244.

as sanctification for life in this world strains under the hermeneutical weight of that discourse's ancient location, with its own contextual limits. Thus, I turn finally to the work of Edward Schillebeeckx as a model for translating the tradition in the contemporary transition from modernity to late (or, perhaps, post-) modernity.

In a popular article he wrote in the late 1970s, not long after completing his massive volume *Christ: The Experience of Jesus as Lord*, Schillebeeckx made a bold proposal about sanctification:

> Holiness is always contextual. Given the current situation of suffering humanity which has now become conscious universally, political love can well become the historically urgent form of contemporary holiness, the historical imperative of the moment, or in Christian terms, the contemporary *kairos* or moment of grace as appeal to believers.[46]

That statement encapsulates key concerns and theological formulations that shaped the lengthy, scholarly book. The issues of suffering humanity, on the one hand, and the grace of God, on the other, constitute the fundamental anthropological problem governing Schillebeeckx's appropriation of the New Testament. In Jesus of Nazareth, God has revealed a positive, unexpected answer to the intractable dilemma of human suffering: God has staked God's honor on identifying with "the happiness and salvation of mankind. God's predestination and man's experience of meaning are two aspects of one and the same reality of salvation."[47] To propose God's predestination, here, strikes me as a creatively traditional way of speaking about the divine nature, allowing for a more contemporary, less metaphysically tinged delivery of the import of the classical notion of human communion with God. Schillebeeckx's conception of this union of divine and human destiny can even enhance the classical notion by conveying a sense of mutuality in the relationship, as opposed to the tendency in the tradition of participation to think predominantly, if not exclusively, in terms of humanity receiving a share in the divine. Here, rather, is a sense of God's free, ongoing share in the human, especially as threatened. Put in a contemporary (at least, American) idiom: God wants to be a part of people's lives. These are lives yearning for life in lifeless conditions.

---

46. Parts of the article "Jerusalem of Benares? Nicaragua of de Berg Athos?" appear translated and retitled in Schillebeeckx, *Reader*, 257–59, 272–74. Here, 272.

47. Schillebeeckx, *Christ*, 628 [639].

In the person and destiny of Jesus of Nazareth, Schillebeeckx argues, God definitively revealed God's cause as the furthering of good and resisting of evil. God identified Godself not only with Jesus' ideals and actions but also with the very person of Jesus. To see Jesus is to see the Father (John 14:9b) and thus, Jesus is "God's countenance turned towards man, the countenance of God who is concerned for all men, especially and concernedly for the humble of the earth, all those who are crucified."[48] Jesus' destiny does not end with his resurrection from the dead; rather, God's affirmation of Jesus continues in God's self-revelation as "solidarity with the people." Jesus' suffering had no value in itself. Only as suffering for a cause, for the sake of the kingdom of God, in the resistance against injustice, does Jesus' suffering bring redemption. In the resurrection, Jesus' cause for humanity is affirmed as God's cause: "For the name of God is 'the one who shows solidarity with his people,' and this people suffers."[49]

From this can be drawn the implication for what it means to participate in, to be a part of, God's life—that is, to be holy. The sanctified person suffers not for the sake of suffering but for the sake of the reign of God, for the sake of that which will ultimately prevail. Schillebeeckx identifies this type of suffering with "sacrificial love." Love includes a capacity for suffering, and such suffering contributes meaning to life. Indeed, Schillebeeckx considers suffering for the good, for righteousness, as essential to a truly human world. The Christian community is the sacrament (the corporeal manifestation) of God's ongoing gracious action on behalf of humanity: "In the church community the future of Jesus, endorsed by his resurrection, is at the same time a remembrance of his life."[50] This remembrance (*anamnesis*) is not a matter of literally imitating what Jesus did but, rather, of responding to one's own situation on the basis of an intense experience of God. Filled with the Spirit of God (now the Spirit of Jesus), Christians share in his Abba experience and his mission for the kingdom of God with a readiness to suffer for the cause of humanity. The history or story of Jesus only lives because of the history of the Christian community, the disciples who follow him: "Thus resurrection, the formation of a community and the renewal of the world in accordance with the life-style of the kingdom of God (in a particular set of circumstances) form a single event with a

48. Schillebeeckx, *Christ*, 628 [639].

49. Schillebeeckx, *Christ*, 630 [640].

50. Schillebeeckx, *Christ*, 630 [641].

spiritual and a historical side."[51] This altogether points to the nature and function of worship in Christian life.

By seeing the resurrection and the founding of the church as one integral event, Schillebeeckx links the sanctified life of the church with the life of the Sanctified One. The presence of Jesus in the Spirit makes Jesus the Christ the one who sanctifies the people of God. This people's mission is to the world, a mission of liberation (the reform of societal structures) and redemption (participation in the already-but-not-yet-fully-realized life of the reign of God) in the one history of salvation of all people together: "[H]uman salvation is only salvation, being whole, when it is universal and complete. There cannot really be talk of salvation as long as there is still suffering, oppression and unhappiness alongside the personal happiness that we experience, in our immediate vicinity or further afield."[52] This thought resonates with and augments Schillebeeckx's early work, *Christ, the Sacrament of the Encounter with God*, wherein he argued that the body of the church and the heavenly body of Christ are "sacramentally identical," with sacramental liturgies serving as "markers, milestones," for the entire Christian life as worship, an ongoing, corporate act of communion with God. The moral life is the concrete shape that communion takes in the world.[53] Christ's act of redemption "remains a permanent actuality in which we become involved through the sacraments. All turns upon a participation in the grace of Christ."[54] In his later work Schillebeeckx's exposition of the spiritual and historical dimensions of both the originating event of Christianity and the ongoing life of the church ground the necessity of both mysticism (liturgy, prayer, contemplation) and politics (intense social efforts) for holiness in contemporary life. And that life, if faithful to the gospel and the world to which it always announces salvation amidst the injustices of every age, is a life of contrasts.

---

51. Schillebeeckx, *Christ*, 631 [642]. In response to an investigation by Vatican doctrinal officials Schillebeeckx elaborated on this understanding of the resurrection in relation to the origins of the church. See Schillebeeckx, *Interim Report*, 80–89 [92–102].

52. Schillebeeckx, *Christ*, 717–20 [726–27].

53. Schillebeeckx, *Christ the Sacrament*, 72–73, 183, 200.

54. Schillebeeckx, *Chris, the Sacrament*, 180.

At the Intersection of Liturgy and Ethics:
The Contrast Experience

As we have seen for Schillebeeckx, while much suffering in the world is unjust and unnecessarily inflicted, still, all instances of suffering are not evil. Indeed, endemic to human experience is the "refractoriness" or resistance of reality to people's ideas, plans, or expectations, let alone the refractoriness of evil and meaninglessness. Knowledge requires struggle with such resistance, and reason (as Kant demonstrated) is aware of its limits in perceiving the object.[55] The latter, according to Schillebeeckx, opens up a "space" for human creativity. This is especially true in the ethical and mystical spheres of life, for in both these areas people encounter aspects of their lives and world that exceed the bounds of any scientific or technical explanation. In the mystical aspect, which includes prayer, liturgy, and creeds, people play—engage in "unproductive" activity—with the remembrance (*anamnesis*) of God's faithfulness and in expectation of God's final fulfillment of that faithfulness (*eschatology*). In the ethical sphere people continuously encounter others—individuals, groups, systems—in situations that resist simple identification with what has been done before and, thus, require new decisions for action. Moreover, as we touched on early in this study, the ethical takes priority over the mystical insofar as prayer and liturgy become delusion or even support for unjust ideologies if not performed with an awareness of the ethical concerns that always press the *humanum*.

The intersection of the mystical and the ethical Schillebeeckx most poignantly articulates as the negative or critical experience of contrast, a concept he has developed and revisited over the decades of his writing. In *Church*, the final book of his trilogy, he undertakes to "radicalize"[56] what he has previously proposed about the concept in a way that serves the highly apologetic quality of a book directed to an increasingly unchurched or even atheistic society. In presenting the contrast experience here, however, I prefer to follow earlier writings, some of which were pastorally addressed to audiences of more religiously engaged Christians.

The contrast experience has two facets. (1) First, a Christian who is poor or oppressed or who has committed himself or herself in solidarity with these people experiences the acute absence of God in a situation of injustice. This situation of suffering contrasts negatively with the divine

55. See Schillebeeckx, *Christ*, 812–15 [817–19].
56. Schillebeeckx, *Church*, 5 [5].

love for humanity one has known in prayer, liturgy and contemplation. (2) The Christian acts, then, to end the alienation. By thus acting, he or she experiences "precisely in political love and resistance against injustice an intense contact with God, the *presence* of the liberating God of Jesus."[57] It is in ethical practice on behalf of the suffering that the Christian *experiences* the grace of God, for God's grace is the very activity of bringing about the salvation of people. In this way, Schillebeeckx speaks of the presence of God. One experiences the absence of God in the overwhelming instance of suffering, but in the effort to defeat that suffering, one experiences God's presence. If one wants to know God, one engages in God's practice—the ongoing effort for the wholeness and happiness of people. Whereas Schillebeeckx describes the contrast experience as "the possibility of a new experience of Transcendence,"[58] it may well also be considered, in terms of the traditional doctrine of sanctification, as a new form of empirical evidence that the sanctified person participates in the divine life. The love the politically engaged Christian expends on behalf of suffering humanity discloses his or her participation in the life and love of God.

Contrast experiences can only occur if indeed Christians practice forms of mysticism in their lives. Schillebeeckx states directly, "Christianity without God is the end of all Christianity."[59] The various ways in which God comes explicitly to Christians in their religious traditions of contemplation, prayer, and sacramental liturgy (all of which include engagement with Scripture) are the experiences that give rise to a critical commitment to humanity in the world. Thus, Schillebeeckx's promotion of political holiness, far from discarding the mystical and liturgical aspects of the life of faith, has an irreducible need for the latter: "Politics without prayer or mysticism quickly becomes grim and barbaric; prayer or mysticism without political love quickly becomes sentimental and irrelevant interiority."[60]

Schillebeeckx considers "mediated immediacy" the most adequate expression of the mystery of God as salvation of humanity and, therefore, as the basis for understanding the nature of prayer and liturgy, as well as the relationship between these "mystical" aspects and the political aspect of the Christian life.

---

57. Schillebeeckx, *Reader*, 273.

58. Schillebeeckx, *Reader*, 272.

59. Schillebeeckx, *Christ*, 810 [814].

60. Schillebeeckx, *Reader*, 274.

> Between God and our awareness of God looms the insuperable
> barrier of the historical, human and natural world of creation, the
> constitutive symbol of the real presence of God for us. The fact
> that in this case an unmistakable mediation produces immediacy,
> instead of destroying it, is connected with the absolute or divine
> manner of the real presence of God: he makes himself directly and
> creatively present in the medium, that is, in ourselves, our neigh-
> bors, the world and history. This is the deepest immediacy that I
> know.[61]

This principle of mediated immediacy we have already seen operative in
Schillebeeckx's explanation of the contribution that socially-politically active believers bring to the "cause of humanity": They bring a critical awareness that denies any equation of human salvation with politics while also
bringing a passionate commitment to justice based on their search for God
in the world. "[C]hurches are . . . communities which speak *to* God: praying
communities of faith and not just one action group or another, however
praiseworthy such groups may be. Their praxis is the realization of the story
that they tell, above all in the liturgy."[62]

It is the Church's ministry of word and sacrament that provides "the
hermeneutical key or code for reading world history and for bringing it to
greater completion."[63] This hermeneutic is needed so that human beings
can recognize God's presence in history. This is especially true because the
history of the world, fraught with suffering, is not simply equivalent to the
history of salvation. The remembrance of God's salvific action in the life,
death, and resurrection of Jesus—mediated through the words and signs
of liturgy—is at the same time an anticipation of the fullness of liberation
and redemption that God will give to all humanity at the end of history.
The moments of eschatological joy experienced in liturgy become a protest
against injustice when Christians encounter an experience that negatively
contrasts with the vision of God's kingdom. The final healing of humanity
and the world will embrace "both person and society" without doing violence to created reality; God is "the one who transcends all things through
interiorness, who goes beyond all things from within."[64]

---

61. Schillebeeckx, *Christ*, 805 [809].
62. Schillebeeckx, *Church*, 14 [14].
63. Schillebeeckx, *Reader*, 257.
64. Schillebeeckx, *Christ*, 811 [815].

Schillebeeckx's contribution to the doctrine of sanctification comes into sharpest focus in the concepts of the negative contrast experience and mediated immediacy. The latter concept brings new sophistication to the theological attempt to explain the sacramentality of the world and of each human person's experience in the world, as well as situating the Church and its liturgical rites as sacraments of the salvation that God is bringing about in history. The healing and wholeness that God desires is for all aspects of human living. Sanctification is for the whole person, the whole of humanity, and the whole of creation. God has created humanity, the *humanum*, as an open-ended reality, a project in which humanity shares in God's creative but also redemptive love, for the *humanum* is ever threatened by evil and suffering. The contrast experience is the process whereby the Christian works and suffers for the cause of the world's healing and sanctification, which is God's cause, the holy cause. Holiness is a participation in God's very honor, the commitment to the happiness and salvation of people in the complex medium of human experience in history and the world.

Conclusion

While liturgical and pastoral theologians have spilled no small amount of ink on the meaning of the Constitution on the Sacred Liturgy's mandate that full, conscious, and active participation by all the assembled be the priority in the reform and renewal of the liturgy, their concerns have largely been for what that entails within and for the celebration of the rites (especially the Mass) in themselves. When, on the other hand, the notion of participation is parsed along the lines of communion between the individual believer and the triune God, of believers having a role in God's life and God in theirs, of involvement in the salvific project of the crucified and risen Christ, of sanctification through sharing in the mystical body of Christ the head, of holiness realized through taking part in something bigger than oneself (whether mystically or politically), then the import of the Constitution's seventh article comes to the fore: "Christ, indeed, always associates the Church with himself in this great work in which God is perfectly glorified and [people] are sanctified." God's glory consists in humans coming to know and acclaim, ever again or ever further, who the God of Jesus is through taking part in the vision of a new heaven and a new earth, a vision inaugurated in him and sustained, through the historical vicissitudes of suffering humanity, by the power of the Spirit who raised him from the dead, who saves us and raises us up.

7

Poverty of Spirit

Evangelical Symbol Joining Liturgy and Ethics

Introduction

To THINK ABOUT THE relationship between liturgy and ethics is to think
of the latter not as a deductive system of principles for personal and social
behavior, but in broader terms of the images, personages, myths and narratives, symbols and rituals, affections and virtues, as well as principles by
which people shape their views of the world and how to live justly within
it.[1] In my judgment (although, as will soon become evident, not original to
me), such a character-and-virtue approach to ethics[2] makes fundamental
to the problematic of liturgy and ethics the question as to whether and how
there is an *intrinsic relationship* between the two. That theoretical, conceptual question comprises the first half of this essay, beginning with a brief
explication, grounded in the doctrine of Vatican Council II, of the normative nature of claiming an intrinsic relationship between liturgy and ethics
in Scripture and tradition. Then I will follow a review of the contemporary

---

1. See Power and Downey, *Living*, 128–30. In his treatment of the topic, liturgical
theologian Don Saliers means by ethics, "the concrete [Christian] way of life rather than
theoretical interpretations of ethical theory . . . a way of life before God in relation to our
neighbor." Saliers, *Worship*, 172–73.

2. See Bordeyne, "Ethical Horizon," 121–24.

conceptualization of the normative, intrinsic bond between liturgy and ethics, anchored in the decades-long, widely-read work of liturgical theologian Don E. Saliers. Inquiry into the normative, conceptual relationship between liturgy and ethics, given the performative nature of both those theological loci, inevitably points toward challenges to and complementary resources for the affective practice of faith through biblically grounded virtues. The second half of the essay, then, shall explore the potential of one such virtue, poverty of spirit, for theoretically reinforcing and practically enhancing participation in liturgy as formative of a Christian life-ethic.

A Brief, Contemporary Overview of Scripture and Tradition

For well more than a half-century now, the Second Vatican Council's Constitution on the Sacred Liturgy, *Sacrosanctum Concilium* (1963), has been the authoritative traditional source for the theology and practice of the sacraments and other rites of the Catholic Church. Having built upon not only specific liturgical reforms of earlier twentieth-century papacies but also, importantly, a century-long and increasingly ecumenical Liturgical Movement,[3] the constitution quickly came to function as the charter document for sacramental-liturgical renewal in numerous Anglican and Protestant communions, as well. In its inaugural position among the major documents of Vatican Council II, the constitution so integrated the life of the liturgy and the life of the Church as to foster an ecclesiological vision that would reach through all the ensuing documents, especially the two constitutions on the Church: first, the dogmatic one, articulating the normative tradition, and second, the pastoral one, addressing the promise and challenges for not only the Church but all humanity in the practical conditions of the late-modern world.[4]

In the renewal of the Church going forward, *Sacrosanctum Concilium* establishes liturgy as having an integral function, indicated by the subtitle of the opening section of the first chapter, "The Nature of the Sacred Liturgy and Its Importance in the Church's Life." Therein the constitution describes the Church's work of forming and reforming believers as follows:

3. See Haquin, "Liturgical Movement," 696–720; and Wainwright, "Ecumenical Convergences," 721–54.

4. For a recent account, with multiple bibliographical references to earlier works on the topic, see Bullivant, *Mass Exodus*, 142.

the Church must ever preach faith and penance, she must prepare them for the sacraments, teach them to observe all that Christ has commanded, and invite them to all the works of charity, worship, and the apostolate. For all these works make it clear that Christ's faithful, though not of this world, are to be the light of the world and to glorify the Father before men.[5]

The allusion to the Last Discourse in John's Gospel articulates the challenge believers perennially experience in striving to make the gospel the primary source of their worldview, or "lifeworld,"[6] in tension with or even at times opposition to the predominant "social imaginary"[7] of their given place and time. The council fathers couple that Johannine symbol of being in but not of the world (see John 15:19; 17:16) to Christ's ethical exhortation to his hearers in Matthew's Sermon on the Mount who, being "the light of the world," are to practice such "good deeds" as to lead others to acknowledge God. In that acknowledgement is God glorified (Matt 5:14–16). The Constitution immediately goes on to assert:

> Still, the liturgy is the summit toward which the activity of the Church is directed; at the same time, it is the fount from which all the Church's power flows. . . . From the liturgy, therefore, particularly the Eucharist, grace is poured forth upon us as from a fountain; the liturgy is the source for achieving in the most effective way possible human sanctification and God's glorification, the end to which all the Church's other activities are directed.[8]

That same paragraph speaks of the Eucharist as providing the ongoing "renewal" of the covenant between God and the faithful, so as to be "compelled" by Christ's love, which "sets them on fire." Believers need to be compelled, need constantly to be renewed, promoted, and empowered for their mission in but not of the world.

And yet, the New Testament gives evidence of how even the liturgical assembling on the Lord's Day can fail to accomplish its eucharistic purpose. Paul bluntly asserts to the wealthier Corinthians, who drink and dine in

5. Paul VI, *Sacrosanctum Concilium*, no. 9.

6. For an explanation and application of the concept of "lifeworld," whereby Jürgen Habermas theorizes the importance of "the immediate milieu," of "intersubjective communication and action" through which "the individual social actor" engages social, political, and cultural systems, see Power and Downey, *Living*, 10–12.

7. For discussion of this concept, see further below.

8. Paul VI, *Sacrosanctum Concilium*, no. 10.

disdainful disregard for the poor, late-arriving laborers of the community, that their ethical failure is likewise a mystical (sacramental) one: "When you come together it is not really to eat the Lord's supper" (1 Cor 11:20). Likewise, the Johannine tradition that professes Jesus as the bread of life and recounts him during the Last Supper commanding his disciples to mutual love and service, finds itself obliged in a subsequent epistle to admonish: "Those who say, 'I love God,' and hate their brothers or sisters are liars; for those who do not love a brother or sister whom they have seen, cannot love God whom they have not seen" (1 John 4:20; see also John 6:35; 13:14–15, 34–35). What becomes evident in primordial Christian tradition is that human sanctification is anything but a matter simply between the individual and God; rather, God's glorification comes through a way of life, liturgical and ethical, that is irreducibly communal, interpersonal, and social.

What the Johannine and Pauline traditions, among others in the New Testament canon, present may be summarized as asserting that the entire Christian life is the worship of God. The way believers live in their bodies, Paul teaches, makes them "a living sacrifice," practicing a holiness that constitutes their "spiritual worship," or as the First Letter of Peter puts it, "living stones" who are being "built into a spiritual house" (Rom 12:1; 1 Pet 2:5). J.-M.-R. Tillard comments on 1 Peter: "The whole letter is permeated by the conviction that this holiness—the form taken by life led in the 'priestly community'—finds its material first of all in a specific relationship with others, even non-Christians."[9] Tillard marshals numerous other New Testament passages, along with patristic letters and homilies engaging them, to show how worship or sacrifice or offering (*leitourgia*) is "no longer just a question of ritual liturgy. It is a question of life *as such*, empowered by the process of its being laid down."[10]

Sacramental liturgy is the means whereby Christians, not least in the very assembling as Christ's body, are empowered by (biblical) word and symbols making explicit for them the mystery of salvation God's Spirit is working out so often in hidden or scattered ways across their lives and in wider society.[11] The people of God must continuously come together on the Lord's Day to gather and share the fragmented stories of their lives as a participation in the human story of God.[12] Hence the Constitution on

9. Tillard, *Flesh*, 23.

10. Tillard, *Flesh*, 97. See also 105–7.

11. See Morrill, *Divine Worship*, 5–9; and Morrill, "Liturgy," 187–206.

12. Here I borrow from the theory and symbolic terminology of Edward Schillebeeckx, as shall be discussed and documented further below.

the Sacred Liturgy's rhetoric for the liturgy, especially the Eucharist, as the source (or fountain) and summit of the Church's mission in its members. The time of the Church is an ongoing advent wherein believers proclaim the death of the Lord until he comes (see 1 Cor 11:26), actively await a new heaven and a new earth (see 2 Pet 3:13; Rev 21:1), variably realizing and falling short of that proclamation and promise in their lives, personally, ecclesially, and societally.

The Conceptual Problematic: Thinking with Don E. Saliers

Within a decade after Vatican Council II, the relationship between liturgy and ethics became a topic of investigation for a certain number of sacra-mental-liturgical theologians and, to a lesser extent, theological ethicists. Among the more notable theorists of the question to emerge in that period was the Methodist theologian of liturgy and spirituality, Don E. Saliers. Writing in the latter 1970s, Saliers found the topic in need of conceptual clarity, not only in light of societal changes that had significantly impacted the perception and even viability of formal church worship, but also due to what he observed, with dismay, to be theological and pastoral-liturgical strategies focused on personal feelings and social themes-of-the-moment. Saliers's essay proved programmatic for addressing anew the problem and then pressing a normative claim, resonant with *Sacrosanctum Concilium* and influenced by his Wesleyan heritage, founded upon ancient tradition's joining of the glorification of God with the sanctification of people.

Saliers' theological vision, which he advanced and critically revisited in the 1990s,[13] is a holistic one for Christian life in community, an ongoing process of liturgically forming and reforming affections and virtues that dispose the faithful to assess and act ethically in concrete life-contexts and situations.

> How we pray and worship is linked to how we live—to our de-sires, emotions, attitudes, beliefs and actions. This is the norma-tive claim of all communities intending to be faithful to Scripture and the inner norms of the Church's declaration of faith. Yet how we pray and worship is, empirically considered, often radi-cally in conflict with how we live. Such is the description of what is the case sociologically. Upon this gap between the "rhetoric" and the "reality" of liturgical worship we have recently had no

13. See Saliers, *Worship*, 171–90; and Saliers, "Afterword," 209–24.

> end of commentary. . . . The fundamental conviction undergird-
> ing [this essay] is that, properly considered, there is an internal,
> conceptual link between liturgy and ethics. At the foundations of
> Christian faith and throughout Jewish teachings, liturgy and eth-
> ics are bound together internally. That is, the link is not causal
> and extrinsic, but conceptual and intrinsic. Our problem is how to
> articulate this without doing injustice to the complexity of other
> relationships between liturgy and ethics which can be described.[14]

Saliers's insistence on the "conceptual and intrinsic" relationship between liturgy and ethics "as a concrete way of life before God with neighbor"[15] is not unlike Catholic moral theologian Pierre Bordeyne, building on the work of the late William Spohn,[16] enlisting the parable of the Good Samaritan: Luke frames the parable with the dialogue between Jesus and the lawyer concerning the twofold commandant of love for God and neighbor and Christ's concluding command, "Go and do likewise" (Luke 10:37), thereby prompting reflection on who the believer might become in follow-ing this Jesus.[17] Formation of character in the virtues thereby constitutes the practical basis for ethics in Christian life, the empowerment of which, analogously to Luke's narrative, comes through a "*transforming* encounter with the risen Christ," subjectively experienced in prayerful word and sac-rament, especially the Eucharist.[18]

What Saliers means by insisting on the relationship between liturgy and ethics as conceptual and intrinsic may further be understood by con-sidering what he is arguing *against*. Saliers opposes efforts in theory and practice to forge an "extrinsic and causal" link between the two, about which he comments: "This approach is reinforced by the easy assumptions of sociology and psychology of religion in our time."[19] Saliers was writing at the end of an era, a decade after the social and cultural upheavals initiated in the latter 1960s, wherein relevance and practicality (action and results) in the urgency for social change put into question the *utility* of doing lit-urgy or other traditional religious practices.

14. Saliers, "Liturgy," 174.

15. Saliers, "Liturgy," 174.

16. See Spohn, *Go*, 87–99.

17. Bordeyne, "Ethical Horizon," 125. For a discussion of parable as the narrative type that brings to the fore the ethical consequences and implications of the biblical "great story" (of creation, covenants, and Christ), see Power and Downey, *Living*, 62–63.

18. Bordeyne, "Ethical Horizon," 125.

19. Saliers, "Liturgy," 174.

While not referencing him in that 1979 essay, Saliers greatly admired and drew from the work of the Orthodox liturgical theologian Alexander Schmemann,[20] who in books and essays produced from the 1960s to early 1980s regularly denounced efforts, both academic and pastoral, to make liturgy more "relevant" and useful for people's lives. Schmemann bemoaned what he characterized as turning liturgy into a means of "help" with people's psychological and personal growth, while he excoriated new, experimental liturgies thematically addressing social-political issues and conflicts of the day.[21] This, to employ Saliers's language, is to distort liturgy into "an instrument to get things done,"[22] stripping it of its very nature—as praise and thanksgiving, anamnesis and epiclesis, invocation and beseeching, intercession and lament—and thereby of the divine grace it offers humanity: "Liturgy is the nonutilitarian enactment of the drama of the divine-human encounter, made flesh in the way of Jesus Christ. At the heart of this is our acknowledgement and our response to the divine initiative. The life of worship is drawn into the divine goodness."[23]

One way to round out this review of the conceptual and normative interrelatedness of liturgy and ethics is to note how, in revisiting the question in the 1990s, Saliers argues that Christian liturgy is "not merely *cultus*," while Christian moral norms and social-ethical practices are "never simply or 'purely' ethical."[24] Those assertions align with my own argument, above, for the entire Christian life as worship of God, a participation in God's biblically revealed, inspired desires for the world. The explicit, graced encounter with God in *sacramental-liturgical* worship constitutes its irreducible necessity for the Church and its members to carry out their life-mission in and for the world. Similarly, Catholic theologians David Power and Michael Downey's proposal of the "Christian ethic" as a way of life grounded

---

20. "The fountainhead for many of us working on relations between Christian liturgy and theology remains Alexander Schmemann . . ." Saliers, *Worship*, 13. Major liturgical theologians across a range of ecclesial affiliations have built so strongly on the Orthodox Schmemann's work that some characterize them as together comprising a particular "school" of liturgical theology. For recent engagement of his work, see Taylor, *We Give Our Thanks*.

21. See, for examples, Schmemann, *For the Life*, 124–26; and Schmemann, *Eucharist*, 9–10. In similar fashion, German Lutheran theological ethicist Bernd Wannenwetsch made a critical analysis of the Political Night Prayer initiative in 1968 Cologne. See Wannenwetsch, *Political Worship*, 31.

22. Saliers, *Worship*, 177.

23. Saliers, *Worship*, 189.

24. Saliers, *Worship*, 189, 172. See also Saliers, "Liturgy," 174.

in trinitarian faith comes through "a doxological theology steeped in and shaped by the worship of the Christian people."[25]

A Christian moral theology based on virtues and character-formation depends upon the grace-dimension of liturgy, the utterly gratuitous gift of God's favor, God's loving care and mercy, experienced in moments of genuine revelation through specific symbols, words, gestures, and person-ages that (re)orient how believers venture into life's challenges with and for others. Encounter or accompaniment with others, both in liturgy and wider life, may be either exciting, inviting, and consoling or threatening, off-putting, and even scary; and this is so whether the Other be a fellow creature—most often but not only fellow human(s)—or God, whether apo-phatically or in the person of Christ Jesus.[26] Openness to divine epiphany through participation in the full range of modalities[27] of liturgical prayer (word, symbols, actions) shapes and reshapes over the time of life, in its continuities and disruptions, the affections and virtues—gratitude, truth-fulness, compassion, solidarity—out of which believers discern their ethi-cal commitments and choices.[28]

Still, we must not overstate the continuity between the affections and virtues fostered through participation in sacramental worship and their concretely being lived out in an ethics of character, as if the two are smoothly realized in human discernment and action, individual and social. Here the practical relationship between liturgy and ethics comes into play. Saliers describes this in terms of the "gap" between what is being liturgi-cally enacted and the actual ways Christians live.[29] This reality, nonetheless, discloses a further intrinsic characteristic in the tradition. Recognition of the practical gap, itself, is one of the graces of sanctification—that is, part of the formation of character—participation in the liturgy may effect:

> The moral struggles and the awareness of ethical dispute and con-flict are, if we have ears to hear and eyes to discern, found in the readings, the Psalms, and in the broken symbol at the heart of the Eucharist. Furthermore, if preaching is honest and deeply honed

25. Power and Downey, *Living*, 130. At the outset of their text, the authors make ex-plicit that by worship they mean "liturgy [as] the source and summit of our participation in the Divine Communion." Power and Downey, *Living*, xii.

26. See Power and Downing, *Living*, 116. See also Bordeyne, "Ethical Horizon," 131.

27. See Saliers, "Liturgy," 175; and Saliers, *Worship*, 173.

28. On liturgy as formation in discernment, see Bordeyne, "Ethical Horizon," 123–24.

29. Saliers, "Liturgy," 179.

in the Scripture and contemporary human experience, the tensions in attempting to live out our religious ethics are made clear and taken up into the sacramental character of prayer. Ultimately this is a liberating feature of authentic liturgy: our moral anguish and our inabilities to live in accordance with the demands of the gospel are named and placed in an eschatological hope.[30]

In his initial essay, Saliers described the gap as a "dialectic" built right into the traditions of liturgical prayer.[31] His fuller elaboration, as quoted here from his book-length work a dozen years later, is consistent with this notion of a dialectical tension that can and, indeed, *should* arise in the doing of liturgy itself, bearing the potential for both spiritual and ethical conversion in the participants. Precisely on this dialectical tension between liturgy and ethics the very *authenticity* of sacramental worship depends—a claim, I would note, that harkens back to the primordial normative teaching in Paul's First Letter to the Corinthians. The liturgy only exists in the practice of actual communities of faith, thereby making the normative—intrinsic and conceptual—relationship between liturgy and ethics contingent on whether the assembled "have ears to hear and eyes to discern."

Thus, once the academic theologian has positively asserted the intrinsic relationship between liturgy and ethics within the entire Christian life as worship of God and negatively ruled out manipulating liturgy for utilitarian ends so that the nature, function, and elements of liturgy can exercise their proper character-forming potential for its participants, then "the complexity of other relationships between liturgy and ethics"[32] inevitably come to the fore. Writing two decades after his original article on liturgy and ethics, Saliers addressed four "clusters" of concerns that constructive critics of his programmatic thesis gradually raised.[33] One may fairly summarize the common underlying problem to be other socially—including, in specific contexts, *ecclesially*—functional attitudes, policies, practices, prejudices, priorities, as well as primary narratives, symbols, and rituals, taking prerogative over and thereby compromising the character and virtue-forming capacities of Christian liturgy. In a word, individuals and groups and even the ministerial leadership at sacramental worship may be practicing the

---

30. Saliers, *Worship*, 174.

31. Saliers, "Liturgy," 179.

32. Saliers, "Liturgy," 174. This is Saliers's disclaimer at the end of his original programmatic statement; see above.

33. See Saliers, "Afterword," 211–18.

liturgy, to invoke Charles Taylor's concept, according to a "social imaginary" at odds with the affections and virtues liturgical celebration of the paschal mystery would foster. Taylor astutely argues that people largely do not practice their lives according to abstract theories but, rather, by "imagining" and participating in their social surroundings according to images, stories, symbols (including historical or contemporary personages), etc.[34] Such philosophical conceptualization accords with Saliers's assertion of affections and virtues as the basis for how people practice their ethical lives.[35]

The notion of dialectic, then, pertains beyond the dynamics *within* liturgy itself. Indeed, academic or second-order theology can only adequately serve the primary or first-order practice of the faith in specific contexts by attending to the ongoing, mutually confirming *and* correcting dialectic *between* communal performance of liturgy (and other spiritual or mystical practices) and moral-ethical engagement in everyday life and society. Theorizing that problematic has been the contribution of contemporary practical fundamental theologies. Since the last third of the twentieth-century, political theologians in the North and liberation theologians in the South have explained Christian faith as a praxis of liturgy and ethics, mysticism and politics.[36] The relationship between these two distinct categories of practice is necessarily dialectical, that is to say, mutually impacting, in ways that inevitably entail conversion of Christian individuals and institutions, including the liturgy,[37] due to the fact that, true to biblical tradition, believers ever find themselves called to a life in but not of the world.

European political theologian Johann Baptist Metz has compellingly argued that the praxis of Christian faith is redemptive to the extent that it empowers people with virtues capable of countering and correcting forces that dehumanize themselves and others personally, interpersonally, and socially, while upbuilding what enables life to flourish therein.[38] Over against the dominant European (and I would add, American) social forces of globalized capitalism, consumerism, and secularism that accelerate individualism and social-ethical apathy, mystical-liturgical practices

34. See Taylor, *Secular Age*, 171–76.

35. On Eucharist fostering an "eschatological imagination," see Bieler and Schottroff, *Eucharist*, 4–30, 41–50, 165–76.

36. See Metz, *Emergent Church*, 63; and Metz, *Faith*, 29; Gutiérrez, *Theology of Liberation*, 143–56; Schillebeeckx, *Christ*, 40–47 [55–61]; and Schillebeeckx, *Church*, 14, 30–33 [14–15, 31–33].

37. See Morrill, *Anamnesis*, 54–60, 128–31.

38. See Metz, *Emergent Church*, 4–8.

enable capacities for sorrow and joy, mourning and expectation, generosity and gratitude, friendship and loyalty, and solidarity with others in their suffering and struggles. Insofar as Metz calls these grace-inspired capacities "messianic virtues," an affinity with Saliers's conceptualization of the normative relationship between liturgy and ethics is readily evident. What Metz brings to Saliers's concern for the practice of liturgy to be authentic, that is, for it to reveal the gap between the faith being celebrated through word and sacrament and the failure of or resistance to live by the virtues revealed therein, is what he identifies as the fundamental evangelical virtue upon which all others depend: poverty of spirit.

For the (somewhat shorter) second half of this paper, I will pursue with Metz the virtue of poverty of spirit. If Saliers has convincingly argued for the intrinsic and conceptual relationship between liturgy and ethics, Metz's theology of the poverty of spirit would seem to be the virtue most fundamentally bonding the two and, thus, the key to narrowing the gap between how Christians practice liturgy and how they live ethically. As an evangelical or messianic virtue, poverty of spirit is a participation in divine grace. The human means for all such divine participation is symbolism which, to follow the seminal work of Paul Ricoeur, encompasses elements and objects of the natural world, human corporeality, persons and historical events, and, perhaps most prominently for constructing meaning, word or language itself.[39] In Christian tradition, poverty of spirit is one such symbol. We need only consider how readily the symbolic phrase, "Blessed are the poor in spirit," gives rise to a broad range of thoughts, invitations, quandaries, or avoidances in those who hear or speak it. In short, I am asserting that the title of a virtue such as poverty of spirit is a symbol generative of the sort of life-ethic to which it points.

In what follows, I start by considering, with the help of Gustavo Gutiérrez, the multivalent symbolism of the word poverty, so as to clarify both its necessarily negative connotations and evangelical promise. Fundamental attention to this symbol is the hallmark of liberation theologies. Metz himself recounts how much he learned from the primary, lived theology he witnessed in visiting Latin American communities, as well as from the second-order theology produced therewith.[40] Then shall follow an investigation of Metz's rich theology, biblical with a practical intent, of

39. See Ricoeur, *Symbolism*, 10–16; and Ricoeur, *Interpretation Theory*, 53–63.
40. See Metz, *Emergent Church*, 82–94; and Morrill, *Anamnesis*, 46, 55–57.

poverty of spirit. Finally, I shall take up the practical potential by relating the symbol, and its referent virtue, to the celebration of liturgy today.

Poverty of Spirit: An Invigorating Symbol for Christian Life and Liturgy

One of the principles of Latin American liberation theology, from which the Northern church can benefit, is its expectation that the biblical word of God promises life-changing power when read through the lens of suffering humanity who, after all, are the fundamental object of God's love throughout both testaments.[41] This hermeneutical lens radicalizes Christian faith by confirming the urgency of human need in real contexts, such that any symbol in the tradition can only be effectively engaged in real (versus some imagined "spiritual") life by attending first to its situation in nature and history.[42] To develop an effective theology of poverty of spirit, then, requires attention to the historical realities of human poverty, such that the spiritual power for redemption and liberation in the paradoxical poverty Christ announces in the Beatitudes (see Matt 5:1–12; Luke 6:20–26) may become clearer, if not compelling.

Gustavo Gutiérrez, in his landmark work, *A Theology of Liberation*, came to distinguish three types of poverty evident in contemporary Christian faith practiced in the material, social conditions of Latin America.[43] At the base is privation, *material poverty*, which widely takes physical, cultural, and psycho-social forms, reducing those in its throes to nonpersons, subhuman and insignificant. While subjected to what can only be judged scandalous living conditions, Gutiérrez notes, the poor nonetheless have great gifts, virtues, to share among themselves and toward those not oppressed, even the oppressors.[44] The virtues practiced by the poor are characterized by finding one's balance not just (or even) in one's self but in relation to others, which so often is a matter of profound conversion. But such giftedness among the poor is born of another type of poverty, quite different in nature. *Spiritual poverty*, Gutiérrez explains, is a life approached

41. See, for example, Gutiérrez, *Power*, 94–96.

42. See Gutiérrez, *Theology of Liberation*, 83–97.

43. The following rehearsal of Gutiérrez's three-part analysis of poverty is based on Gutiérrez, *Theology of Liberation*, 163–71.

44. For another example of this widely held observation-cum-testimony to the virtues of the poor, see Sobrino, *No Salvation*, 17, 52–53, 62–63.

in complete dependence upon the love of God, life as a child of God, totally open to God, available to hearing the word of God, with a desire that God be one's sole sustenance. This is not passive acceptance of one's material, socially inflicted conditions but, rather, an embracing of reality empowered by the Spirit of God.[45]

Finally, Gutiérrez delineates a third type of poverty, the *evangelical poverty* practiced in solidarity with those who suffer privation, a lived commitment and protest against scandalous poverty. What makes this poverty evangelical is the willingness to risk all one has and is in a Christ-like *kenosis*, a voluntary empowerment out of loving solidarity with the poor. This characteristic of risking all is likewise essential to Jon Sobrino's "principle of mercy," an attitudinal life-structure of making the other's pain one's own, such that one is moved to respond.[46] When thus practiced in a "de-centered church," in community and against all societal odds, Christian faith becomes "an active hope which unloosens creativity at all levels of human existence."[47] Sobrino developed this concept from his context in El Salvador explicitly for the benefit of North American readers struggling to understand how opting for life in solidarity with the poor proves redemptive and liberating. In what amounts to an invitation, Sobrino describes a conversion of the educated European Christian (that is, himself) who no longer looks only to the crucifix in prayer and liturgy but also to *the crucified people*[48] of our time. Only in that way does the truth of faith become practical or, as Gutiérrez would say, evangelical.

As leading theorist of the new political theology in Europe, Johann Baptist Metz put in fundamental-theological perspective what Sobrino autobiographically called the "slumber" of (individualistic, pure-reason-focused) first-world, "progressive" theology.[49] Metz argued that theology was being done in a strange, idealist-transcendental enclosure ignoring twentieth-century's human catastrophes, forgetting Auschwitz. The latter stands as a symbol for Europeans analogous (but only that!) to the crucified people of El Salvador. As an antidote to this bourgeois, self-absorbed

---

45. Elsewhere in his writings, Gutiérrez describes the eucharistic celebrations in the poor communities of Latin America as their character-empowering share in Christ's paschal mystery. See Gutiérrez, *Power*, 107.

46. Recall the similar argument by Bordeyne and Spohn, earlier.

47. Sobrino, *Principle*, 6, 21–22.

48. See Sobrino, *Principle*, 49–57.

49. See Sobrino, *Principle*, 1–3.

Christianity, Metz proposes poverty of spirit. Whereas he produced a little monograph by that title in 1968,[50] one finds that he radicalized the entire notion in a 1990 essay, "*Theologie als Theodizee*."[51] To my thinking, insofar as Christianity is a religion of deliverance and redemption, Metz was quite right in centering the question of theology's validity, and thus, very viability, on the problem of suffering, of evil's manifestation in sinfulness both conceived as a broad human condition and recognized in particular human acts, corporate and individual.

Metz argues that theodicy, as a genuine questioning of God in light (or, perhaps, the dark) of suffering, receded from theology as Augustine turned the question away from God and back onto humanity. Metz perceives Augustine seeking to resolve the problems a centuries-persistent Marcionism was causing for orthodox faith:

> [U]sing a gnostic dualism of a creator and redeemer God, [Marcion] tried to close the open flank of the theodicy question, which accompanies the historical development of biblical discourse about God in the form of crying-out and inconsolable expectation. The early church decisively rejected this offer.[52]

Augustine, however, shifted the blame onto freely, badly acting humans, effectively replacing theodicy with "anthropodicy." Still, Metz questions, in the end whether Augustine did not draw a Marcion-like dualism back into theology with the notion of predestination of the elect and the damned. With this came a certain timeless quality to salvation, the salvation of the eternal soul, leaving time itself, that is, human history, something to be circumvented and, ultimately, escaped.

As a fundamental corrective (with practical intent), Metz proposes an "Israelite-Biblical Paradigm" for theodicy. Christian theology should not turn to Israel only for its "faith" while deriving its "spirit" from the Greeks, but, rather, should embrace the Israelite spirit as well.[53] Unlike Platonic anamnesis, Israel's is a historical "remembrancing,"[54] a liturgically-grounded

---

50. See Metz, *Poverty of Spirit*.

51. Metz, *Passion*, 54–71.

52. Metz, *Passion*, 59.

53. Metz, *Passion*, 64. Here Metz takes issue with a thesis Joseph Ratzinger asserted in "*Eschatologie und Utopie*."

54. This English neologism translates the German *Eingedenken*, which the translator explains Metz derived from the adverb *eingedenk*, meaning "in remembrance of," as used in the church's eucharistic prayer. See Metz, *Passion*, 181n10.

remembering with the God of the covenant that refuses to forget history, to erase its victims:

> What is it that distinguished pre-Christian Israel, what is it that distinguished this small, culturally rather insignificant and politically humble desert folk from the glittering high cultures of its time: In my view it was a particular sort of defenselessness, of poverty, in a certain sense Israel's incapacity successfully to distance itself from the contradictions, the terrors and chasms in its life.[55]

Against the temptation to embrace alien myths and fables—whether for historic Israel, those of Babylonian or Greco-Roman deities and humans, or for contemporary Christians, the totalizing myths of modern progress or the scientific elimination of suffering—Metz asserts: "Poverty of spirit is the foundation of any biblical discourse on God."[56] To practice poverty of spirit is to *suffer unto God* (*Leiden an Gott*) in constant, time-limited expectation. The Church thereby "exposes itself . . . shows an open flank," united with suffering humanity, "a pathic monotheism, with a painfully open eschatological flank."[57]

With his theology of remembrancing, of anamnesis and anticipation, Metz points toward time and, thus, eschatology, as being of the essence of Christian liturgy. This requires thinking and practicing liturgy as not only, nor even primarily, incarnational but rather paschal, grounded in the paschal mystery.[58] The problem with an incarnational-sacramental approach to liturgy is that it can foster a static image of salvation as completed in past events. Liturgy and ethics become a matter of recalling all Christ suffered "for me" such that I resolve, once again, to do better, to avoid sin and to try to imitate him and, perhaps, the saints. A graceless Pelagianism can seep into Christianity, such that sacraments become rewards to be earned rather than the empowering sources of one's identity with Christ Jesus as a child of God, a Spirit-anointed participant—here and now, mystically and ethically—in the coming reign of God.

> [The biblical concept] *mysterium* refers to a reality that surpasses human thought and is irrevocably bound up with revelation. It is a gracious gift of God. Jesus Christ is the mystery of God into which

---

55. Metz, *Passion*, 65.

56. Metz, *Passion*, 66.

57. Metz, *Passion*, 112, 127.

58. For his critique of scholastic theology in this regard, followed by his constructive, paschal-mystery approach, see Chauvet, *Symbol*, 449–89.

believers are drawn for their salvation. It is present in the community in which it is proclaimed. This is a clearer concept than [the Roman military] *sacramentum* for expressing the salvation-historical dimension of the liturgical celebration. *Mysterium* thus points to both the present and the eschatological dimensions of Christian liturgy as well as to the faith that in the celebration of the liturgy one participates in the divine saving action in Christ.[59]

Celebrated from that latter perspective, sacramental liturgy reveals God's cosmic and historical salvation of the world as an unfinished project in which we can genuinely, actively participate because it is being revealed as ongoing, reaching from and into a future whose promise can be hoped on the basis of God's definitive past deeds, climactically in Jesus.[60]

To perceive how this celebration of mystery in liturgy can be formative of the virtue of poverty of spirit, I conclude by considering one symbol within the service of Good Friday, the midpoint in what the Church considers the most sacred, three-day liturgy of the entire Church Year. Focused on the death of Christ Jesus, the service enacts in mystery what faith discerns to be not the nadir, but the apotheosis of his poverty of spirit, making it the very source, initiated but ongoing, of believer's sharing in that spirit. The dynamic of divine glory and human salvation (justification and sanctification), which is to say, the paschal mystery, is so intensely experienced—revealed and shared—in the proclamation of and communal response to the word of God in the Good Friday service as to make it paradigmatic—theologically and practically—of the liturgy's capacities for deepening in the assembled faithful a mystical participation in Christ Jesus' poverty of spirit, through which all their affections and virtues may practically thrive.

The Open Flank: A Biblical-Liturgical Expansion of Metz's Symbol

Metz's symbolism of Christianity's poverty of spirit as an open flank he seems to have constructed from military imagery of exposure and vulnerability to attack. But as a liturgical theologian, I find the symbol elicits a

59. Gerhards and Kranemann, *Introduction*, 196.

60. "With liturgy being the source and summit of our participation in the Divine Communion, indeed a share in God's own justice, the moral and spiritual life are moored in both memory and in hope." Power and Downey, *Living*, xii. For doctrinal presentation of the eschatological dimensions of the liturgy, see Paul VI, *Sacrosanctum Concilium*, nos. 8, 14, 48.

more theologically profound image steeped in the paschal mystery: the wounded, open side of the dead, crucified Jesus. While depicted in crucifixes looming over the altar of eucharistic sacrifice, the image likewise features in Good Friday's liturgy of the word, wherein proclamation of the pierced Suffering Servant (Isa 53:5) points toward the soldier lancing open the side of Jesus' crucified body.

Among multiple unique features in the passion account of John's Gospel is a detail found at 19:34: a soldier thrusts a lance into the side of Jesus' body to determine if he is dead. Blood and water immediately flow from that completely vulnerable, open flank. Discharge of water and blood is birthing imagery. Jesus' death gives birth to life, is the source of new life for believers and, thus, is the birth of the Church. The moment of Jesus' most abject poverty, having surrendered even his very *spirit* (19:30), proves to be the *hour of his glory*,[61] the culmination of his entire life as given for the life of his believers and, indeed, for the life of the world. Biblical scholar Barbara Reid explains how John theologically constructs this revelation:

> The language of birthing is prominent throughout the whole gospel, culminating with this image of Jesus' death as a birth to new life. The theme is first sounded in the prologue which speaks about those who believe as being born of God (1:12–13). Then, when dialoguing with Nicodemus, Jesus talks about the necessity of being born again/from above (3:3). At the Feast of Dedication (7:38) he speaks about "rivers of living water" that flow from his own and the believer's heart (*koilia*, which is literally, "womb"), foreshadowing John 19:34. At his final meal with his disciples, Jesus likens the pain of his passion to the labor pangs of a woman giving birth (16:21–22). All these texts point forward to John 19:34, where the birth to new life that was begun with Jesus' earthly mission comes to completion in his death.[62]

The cross begins Jesus' ascent to the Father and, with that, his saving Lordship, manifesting his power to give eternal life to all who believe, to all who see "the only true God" (17:3) in this Jesus who finishes the earthly work the Father sent him to do (see 17:4).

The *liturgical* proclamation and sacramental sharing in that saving revelation on Good Friday, however, is not merely the recounting of

---

61. See Schillebeeckx, *Christ*, 398–404 [409–415].

62. Reid, "From Sacrifice," 86. Reid notes that such early Christian bishops as Ambrose of Milan and medieval mystics as Julian of Norwich drew on the Johannine birthing imagery to describe Christ as the mother giving birth to believers.

a completed, past event, one eliciting grief or, to tragic effects in history, even outrage at what was done to Jesus.[63] Good Friday's liturgy of the word, rather, concludes with the assembly of the baptized responding in a series of ten prayerful intercessions reaching out from the center, for the Church's leadership and all its membership, to all who believe in God (starting with the Jewish people, first to receive the covenant), to nonbelievers, and finally to all suffering forms of material poverty. In so doing, the members of the assembly identify themselves with Jesus' earthly mission as now their mission. If the passion constitutes the hour of Jesus' glory, the community, in turn, glorifies God by living in the spirit Jesus gives over at his death, with the water and blood flowing from his pierced side signifying baptism and Eucharist as the life-giving sacraments whereby the Spirit comes powerfully to abide in them.[64]

The great intercessions of Good Friday are poised between the proclamation and reception of the word of God and the sacramental act of venerating the cross. The community does not move directly from gospel to a personal act of liturgical piety; rather, the assembly responds to God's word by giving concrete historical expression to the universal saving will of God and, in so praying, implicating their baptismal identification with that mission in Christ. This is but one way the Good Friday service, at the center of the Easter Triduum, serves as a paradigmatic experience of the weekly Lord's Day liturgy's capacities for drawing participants into the paschal mystery, thereby gracing them with the messianic virtues symbolically expressed in the proclaimed word, shared sacrament, and the prayers arising from the assembly.

Commentators, Protestant and Catholic, agree on early Christianity's association of John 19:34 with the ecclesial sacraments, noting also the passage's relation to the instruction John gives in the First Epistle.[65] The Spirit, the water, and the blood all "testify" (1 John 5:7) to the Christ Jesus from whose flesh they flow, making them the source of the "presence of the absent one."[66] That presence is known mystically in word and sacrament, but these

63. Medieval liturgical celebrations of Good Friday in central and eastern Europe, with preaching and prayers following from the Johannine passion, could result in attacks on Jewish storefronts, synagogues, and persons, even rabbis.

64. See Schnackenburg, *Gospel according to St. John*, 396, 161.

65. See Smith, "John," 1074. Even Rudolph Bultmann recognized the water and the blood as symbols of the two sacraments, while nonetheless denying the verse's authenticity to the Fourth Gospel.

66. Moloney, "Johannine Theology," 1426.

only for the purpose of empowering the members of Christ's mystical body (the church) to know him in their social-ethical lives, wherein the painful eschatological tension of grace and sin takes real form in a faith sustained by a fierce, abiding love lived out in genuine, vulnerable hope. Such comprises a dense summation of the truth proclaimed in the second readings for the seven Sundays of Easter, in which 1 John alternates with 1 Peter and Revelation through the three-year lectionary cycle. Those books, in offering realistic appraisals of not only the consolations but also the challenges of living paschal faith both within the ecclesial community and amidst a troubled, if not oppressive, world, reveal faith in the Risen Crucified One as an ongoing praxis of mysticism and ethics. Embodying joy amidst both concord and conflict, participants realize what Schillebeeckx described as fragmentary moments of the inbreaking of God's reign.[67] Fragments, only, are what we have until the fullness of Christ is revealed. The "already" of biblical Easter faith certainly resides in proclamation of Christ resurrected, but it only lives and breathes in the sacramental body of Christ, the church in its members, for whom their sacramental worship serves as source and summit for living the virtues in concrete behavior. That is what the ancient tradition of mystagogy was all about.[68] And, so, liturgical restoration in the Church may well prove a matter of such mystical-ethical preaching, from and to poverty of spirit, being realized in the global contexts of our day.

Conclusion

Article 7 of *Sacrosanctum Concilium*, having delineated the liturgical presence of the Risen Crucified One in the assembly, presiding minister, proclaimed word, and shared sacrament, proceeds to explain the import of this divine-human presence: "Christ always truly associates the Church with himself in this great work wherein God is perfectly glorified and the recipients made holy. The Church is the Lord's beloved Bride who calls to him and through him offers worship to the eternal Father."[69] Unless taught and practiced with relentless study and proclamation of the biblical God of Jesus, religious rhetoric along the lines of glory and holiness can leave people convinced of sacramental worship's irrelevance to "real life," to their ethical quandaries and moral concerns. But God in Scripture glories in the

---

67. See Schillebeeckx, *Church*, 5–6 [5–6]; and Schillebeeckx, *Christ*, 829–34 [834–39].

68. See Goffredo, *Spiritual* Meaning, 14.

69. Paul VI, *Sacrosanctum Concilium*, no. 7.

salvation, redemption, and deliverance of a humanity whose sanctity entails loving that God wholeheartedly by sharing in that divine, active love among selves and "neighbor." Such practical love is borne of an evangelical poverty of spirit that mourns, comforts, strives for justice, shows mercy, and works for peace. And so, Metz: "It is no accident that 'poverty of spirit' is the first of the beatitudes . . . only through it does God draw near to us."[70] Demonstrating and witnessing to such virtue constitutes the desire to share liturgically in the paschal mystery. The sacramental assembly indeed "calls to her Lord," but in the expectant plea of martyrs, witnesses of faith, hope, and love wedded to Christ in the Spirit. Their response to Christ's assurance, "Yes, I am coming soon," is an urgent, "Amen! Come, Lord Jesus." Thus concludes the reading from Revelation (22:12–14, 16–17, 20) on the Seventh Sunday of Easter. The asking comes from a mystical-ethical poverty of spirit. The sacramental-liturgical empowerment comes in the asking.

70. Metz, *Poverty of Spirit*, 21.

Part IV

Once More, Theory
and Practice

8

Sacramental Liturgy as Negotiation of Power, Human and Divine

Theologizing Sacramental Power[1]

PLEASE ALLOW ME TO begin by saying that I find myself honored and privileged to lead off the annual meeting of the College Theology Society, to be entrusted with addressing the meeting's theme, "Liturgy and Power," in such a way, I hope, as to be informative, perhaps insightful, and even motivational for your collegial work over the next couple days. That decision about and action on the theme on the part of the convention chair and society board is already an exercise of power—albeit not, I trust, in the form of despotic, authoritarian command to you, the members: "You *will* engage the topic of liturgy and power, and you *will* enjoy it!" That would, of course, amount to the power of force and its constant complement, fear, which, frankly, I rather doubt these individuals can affect.

My little (attempt at a) joke here intends to indicate the complexity, but also the theoretical generativity, of the term "power," a concept that, as we all know, has over the past several decades gained broad currency as

---

1. The text of this chapter first served as the opening plenary address for the 62nd Annual Convention of the College Theology Society (June 2016). This accounts for both the style of delivery and discussion of technical concepts presumably familiar to the audience.

an analytical tool in the social sciences and humanities. Without bogging down in a comprehensive literature review, I would just note the influential contribution of Michel Foucault, who argued that theoretical reifications of power, that is, thinking about or promoting power as if "it" were a substantive entity, constitute a fundamental category mistake. Power is not a "thing" to be possessed or deployed but, rather, an activity situated in a social body, a web of relationships, wherein people act with and/or upon others so as to direct their activity (what they think and do with their lives). For this reason, ritual theorist Catherin Bell explains, Foucault argued in terms not of a theory of power (for that would only aid and abet a substantive understanding of power), but rather of an "analytics of power." This approach Bell finds analogous to Clifford Geertz's "poetics of power," whereby power cannot be conceived as "something external to its social workings."[2] Building on those philosophical and social-scientific insights, as well as those of others such as Pierre Bourdieu, Bell made her contribution to analyzing rituals by likewise arguing in terms of ritualization and ritual bodies, that is, for approaching rituals always as specific activities wherein the bodies performing them maintain or become the persons they are within that body of social relations.

If we return, then, to my opening words for this plenary address, the joke lays in my misrepresenting the sort of social body the College Theology Society functionally is and, thus, the type of power the membership affords its officers to practice in relation to them and the Society's purpose and goals. But prior to that little zinger (and therefore probably already forgotten in its wake), I began by laying out what I saw to be the power invested in me and my role or activity in this opening plenary ritual; namely, the power of conveying knowledge, the power of exercising imagination, and the power of motivating this social body in its activity for the next few days.

I speak here of Bell, of course, due to her work's relevance to the field of sacramental-liturgical theology. That hyphenated term is a clumsy effort at indicating that sacraments, like all rituals, are not things but, rather, symbolic activities performed by and for ritual bodies. The Christian term for such activity is liturgy, and so yoking the terms "sacramental" and "liturgical" is the strategy many of us in my field have adopted in order to indicate—to symbolize—the irreducibly praxiological (bodily practical) nature of our subject matter. The sacraments and other rites of the Church only

2. Bell, *Ritual Theory*, 200.

exist in performance by its members, which are clergy and laity. And they are powerful—or not. That last tag, however, points to the disquiet the turn to social-scientific theory has caused (if I may speak in generalities) among the radical orthodox movement and, in various ways, for some other dogmatic and systematic theologians. Is this not dragging the sublime offer of grace down, reducing humans to power struggles rather than elevating their thoughts to the divine power and offer of grace? Do we not make a different category mistake by analyzing the rites of the Church in those terms rather than primarily (if not in some cases, exclusively) thinking about the sacraments metaphysically and ontologically? After all, Christians believe that the unseen, incorporeal God is acting in the Church's sacramental signs for the sanctification of people, in some cases even effecting ontological change in the recipients of those signs (think baptism, confirmation, holy orders) or in the signs themselves (think Eucharist).

Aquinas knew how to think about such power, and did so with undeniable brilliance and reverence. If so disposed, that is, if one's faith yearns for understanding *and* if one understands at least the rudiments of Platonic and Aristotelean philosophy, the reader enters a beautiful "world" in the *Summa Theologia* wherein, as Mark Jordan persuasively demonstrates,[3] the closing Treatise on the Sacraments functions as the teleological lens for understanding all that has unfolded voluminously before. The sacraments are not some extra add-on to the fundamental theology, anthropology, ethics, and Christology Aquinas has worked out philosophically; rather, they are the means whereby God's grace achieves the very end for which humans are created; namely, body-and-soul participation in the very life of God. Aquinas explains how sacraments are thus effective in terms of powers— the principal cause of grace which is God, the divine power in Christ's Passion operative through his humanity, the powers of human body, intellect, and will created so as to be receptive to the healing (justifying) and sanctifying grace in the sacraments, with the Holy Spirit working through them to make believers active members of the body of Christ. That fellowship, activated and sustained through the instrumental power of the sacraments, gives a veritable share in divine charity and goodness that empowers Christians to enact the virtues of faith, hope, and above all love in their lives.

As we know, Aquinas produced his understanding of the sacraments on the basis of both the writings of Church Fathers before him and the elements of the rites as they were practiced in the medieval church of his day.

---

3. See Jordan, *Teaching Bodies*, pt. I.

As I already mentioned, if one enters into his text with a dynamic sense of God's movement (grace) in one's life and the world around one, as well as a fervent and informed participation in and regular exposure to the rites in practice, then study of the *Summa* can indeed prove very powerful. But the problem in seminaries and catechisms was (and, I'm afraid, often still is) that God remained distant, some*body* far away some*place* (heaven). Unless one finds a way to make the constantly invoked term "charity" affectively connect with experiential knowledge of love,[4] then this can all go very dry, very quickly.

Understanding does empower faith. The problem historically was scholasticism's apologetic reduction of such dynamic and sophisticated thought as that of Aquinas into questions and answers about "things"— God, grace, virtues, etc. Seminary education in post-Tridentine Catholicism came to treat the sacraments as a mere unit in dogmatic theology and canon law. Sacraments were surely upheld as powerful, but within a teach-and-tell seminary context forming the ritual bodies of a teach-and-tell clerical culture, in which deferential loyalty and obedience were the key practical, moral, and political virtues. That system persists and has over the past dozen years or so realized a modest but significant resurgence in new members: seminarians taught and told concepts through ritualization in classrooms and chapels forming them as men sent to teach and tell a laity from whom, in turn, obedience is the ideal expectation.

That such a teaching, sanctifying, and governing model of Church was rapidly losing its power on the popular, ground level of European societies by the second half of the twentieth century had become obvious to the redoubtable pastoral intellectuals among the French Dominicans,[5] as well as such Jesuits as Henri de Lubac and Karl Rahner. With his modification of Thomism through a fundamental anthropology of the supernatural existential, Rahner produced a steady stream of essays phenomenologically connecting the Church's traditional sacraments (as well as popular pious practices called sacramentals) to everyday human experience. Rahner was striving to help fellow believers—clergy, vowed religious, and laity—to tap into the divine power immanent in the spectrum of ritualization across

---

4. For arguments for how eucharistic celebration is meant to elevate human friendship into the theological virtue of friendship, see Cooke and Morrill, *Essential Writings*, 109–40, 154–68. Kimberly Hope Belcher has proved insightful commentary on this theme in Cooke's work. See Belcher, "Sacramentality."

5. For a captivating, if not inspirational, account, see O'Meara and Philibert, *Scanning*.

everyday human life and ecclesial traditions.[6] With remarkable efficiency and lucidity, Edward Schillebeeckx in his now-classic book *Christ the Sacrament of the Encounter with God* consolidated the achievements of the renewed pastoral-theological scholarship in patristics and Transcendental Thomism to help the faithful understand and desire the divine meaning to be experienced in the rites and shared in their human lives.[7] Translating the genius of Rahner and Schillebeeckx in a developmental-psychological idiom, Bernard Cooke, in a still widely used textbook, established the deeply traditional principle underlying such phenomenological understanding of the purpose and significance of celebrating the rites by invoking the centuries-old adage: *sacramenta pro populo*.[8] Sacraments are for the benefit of people and only achieve their purpose, let alone "exist" in any real sense, in people's practices of them as integral to their lives of faith and, thus, their lives in the world. The efforts of sacramental theologians, then, have been to renew and augment the power of the rites by making them (more) meaningful for the faithful. I could, as you might well imagine, rehearse a litany of other major contemporary thinkers of liturgy and sacraments, all of whom have striven to connect liturgy and life, to rescue theological reflection and inspiration for sacramental-liturgical practice from banality and irrelevance for late-modern Catholics (and other Christians).[9] Louis-Marie Chauvet, recognizing that urgency, is a standout with his exhaustive semiotic treatment of sacraments as one pole (along with word and ethics) in the symbolic network of the faith of the Church. One extended quote from the French priest-theologian's 550-page tome may serve to convey the theoretical approach and pastoral passion of his project:

> Just as empirical writing is the phenomenal manifestation of an arch-writing that constitutes language as the place where the human subject comes into being, so the sacraments can be appreciated as the empirical manifestation of the *"arch-sacramentality" that constitutes the language of faith*, which is the place where the

6. Each of the more than two dozen volumes of Rahner's *Theological Investigations* include essays addressing various sacraments and sacramental and other practices. Notable monographs include his *Church and Sacraments*.

7. See Schillebeeckx, *Christ the Sacrament*.

8. See Cooke, *Sacraments*, 7.

9. Lest this problem of banal explanations and growing irrelevance of the sacraments be assumed as an exclusively "first" or "developed" world phenomenon, I would direct the reader to similar ecclesial and social challenges now widespread in Catholic India, reported in Gonsalves, *Feet Rooted*.

believing subject comes into being. This arch-sacramentality is a *transcendental condition for Christian existence*. It indicates that *there is no faith unless somewhere inscribed, inscribed in a body*—a body from a specific culture, a body with a concrete history, a body of desire. Baptism, the first sacrament of the faith, shows this well: the plunge into water, together with this "precipitate" of the Christian Scriptures, which is the mention of the names of the Father and the Son and the Holy Spirit, is a metaphor for being plunged into the body of signifiers—material, institutional, cultural, and traditional—of the Church: assembly, ordained minister, sign of the cross on the forehead, book of the Scriptures, confession of faith, remembrance of Jesus Christ and invocation of the Spirit, paschal candle. . . . All these are symbolic elements that are inscribed on the body of every baptized person, his or her *scriptural* body on which they are bestowed as a testament. *One becomes a Christian only by entering an institution and in letting this institution stamp its "trademark," its "character," on one's body.*

The faith thus appears to us as *"sacramental" in its constitution,* and not simply by derivation. Our existence is Christian insofar as it is always-already structured by sacramentality, better still, as it is *always-already inscribed in the order of the sacramental.* It is thus impossible to conceive of the faith outside of the body.[10]

Chauvet's is, as Lieven Boeve points out,[11] a hermeneutical project in dialogue with philosophy and the social sciences with the intention of interpreting the traditional elements of the faith such that it might still be incarnated in history, be lived and professed as meaningful and empowering in the person-bodies of postmodern Christians. His detailed philosophical and social-scientific analyses of the liturgical rites, attuned to history and tradition, Chauvet always carries out with a view to reviving and/or augmenting their pastoral effectiveness, what Tridentine doctrine called their fruitfulness. But that is just another way of saying, to unleash their potential power. The ultimate power source of the liturgy, indeed, is the Spirit of the Risen Crucified One, a participation in the very life of God. Chauvet does treat of this in the latter part of his major book. Still, the burden of the work is not speculative theology but theoretical, critical understanding to renew the relevance and viability of the faith, to motivate its practice, both ritual and ethical.

10. Chauvet, *Symbol,* 154–55.

11. See Boeve, "Theology," 6–14.

Relevance is power. Motivation is power. Knowledge is power. My thinking about and parsing the notion of power along these lines is further influenced by Cooke. Whereas his sacramental theology, both in his writing and tireless teaching in college and pastoral ministry classrooms, comprised exercises in getting people to reflect on how they construct meaning through their life-experiences, in his final writing years, Cooke situated symbolic activity, including Christians' sacramental ritualizing, within the larger question of power, divine and human. This he did through essaying an "Experience-Based Pneumatology," the subtitle of his final scholarly book, *Power and the Spirit of God.* Spirit as the power of divine Word is the theological principle for Cooke's sacramental anthropology, an anthropology irreducibly entailing individual human personhood, interpersonal friendship, and social, communitarian life. For this reason, Cooke argues, Christianity is not meant narrowly to be a religion but, rather, a way of being human, a new creation sacramentally realizing divine love in human sharing.[12] That creativity comes by the power of God's Spirit, yet only in prophetic tension with the whole range of ways humans exercise power.

Cooke organized the book as a series of thematically grouped chapters along a trajectory starting with the forms of human power he argues are most alienating from the divine (force and fear), through a number with varied potential (office, law, fame, wealth, nature, imagination and creativity), to the types of human power most amenable to the divine power revealed in Scripture and tradition (symbol, word, thought, and ritual). That latter symbolic cluster is particularly amendable to mediating the divine Word in creation and as salvation, with the Word's power being the love that is God's Spirit. Insofar as power ultimately entails the ability to motivate and achieve a particular goal, Cooke argues, Christian theological reflection arrives at love as "the affective movement toward 'the good' . . . the ultimate exercise of power, that is, the motivations that lead humans to action."[13] For Christians, that love is definitively revealed in Christ Jesus, especially through word and sacrament. Still, these do not happen in a vacuum, but rather as part of larger communal and societal bodies, including the institutional life of the Church, from the local to Vatican levels.

The conclusion and motivation I draw at the end of this first half of my text is that the relationship between liturgy and power must attend to particular experiences of liturgy, particular exercises of the symbolic ritual

12. See Cooke, *Power,* 27.
13. Cooke, *Power,* 168, 176.

that nonetheless are always contextual within the whole range of other human forms of power Cooke has identified, such as office and law, creativity and imagination, but also force and fear. For addressing my assigned topic at the moment, I take God's power (grace, the love of the Spirit) in and through the pastoral activity of the Church as a theological given, the topic that sacramental theology has covered. The more specifically liturgical-theological questions, on the other hand, necessarily deal with the primary practice of the Church's theology; namely, actual people in communities carrying out the rites. If academic, that is to say, second-order theology, is to get at the experience, then I have found, at least for my own methodology, that I can do so only by means of narrative. For this second half of my text, then, I shall now offer an exercise in my inductive approach to liturgical theology, whereby I first recount in some detail a pastoral narrative that I then analyze on the basis of theological resources and with a view toward making normative theological claims. In this case, the analysis is in terms of the types of power, divine and human, at work and being negotiated in a liturgical event. The goal is to think about the liturgical experience such that thought might motivate, renew, or advance practice, so that thought might, to invoke Paul Ricoeur, return to the symbol.

Description and Analysis of a Liturgical Event: Ash Wednesday

About a decade ago while on faculty at a certain Catholic university, I was part of a team providing the Sunday evening liturgy on one of the university's undergraduate campuses. Two full-time lay campus ministers, two part-time graduate-student ministers, and three priests comprised the team, with the latter presiding and preaching on a rotating basis. As the start of the Lenten season approached that year, I recall our having a conversation about what to do for the Ash Wednesday liturgy. That this service would take place at the same hour as the Sunday Mass—9 PM, which in undergrad time, as we know, is roughly midafternoon—was immediately agreed. The other two priests each begged off involvement, saying they would already have helped at a local parish or on another campus that day. All heads turned to me, who asked whether we needed to be working from the assumption that the service should be a Mass, and if not, whether a priest presiding and preaching in this context would be pastorally optimal. I opined that Ash Wednesday is not a "holy day of obligation" and, therefore, did not necessitate a Mass, and that I believed it presented a prime opportunity for the lay chaplains to preside over a Service of the Word with Distribution of Ashes (an official rite), during which one or even two of them could give homiletic reflections. I was aware that these lay ministers very much desired such opportunities, that the hierarchy's reinforced restriction of the Mass's homily to ordained clergy made awkward the insertion of lay preaching ("reflections") at the beginning or conclusion of Mass (we Catholics are, like all human beings, creatures of habit-memory),[14] and that, in contrast, the order of service for Ash Wednesday would afford the students to hear a word from these ministers at the time to which they were so attuned, namely, after the proclamation of the gospel. Implied in my argument, of course, was the conviction that, in part, the "medium was the message," that is, that hearing about the call to repentance and conversion from a lay man and woman (rather than a clergyman) could well affect the young people in ways both conscious and subconscious. Such affecting, I note here, can be powerful. I explained that we would not be inventing anything, that the Sacramentary (the missal) provided the complete service, which included all the important ritual components of the Liturgy of the Word (communal song, collect prayer, biblical readings and psalmody, homily, prayers of intercession, but with the distribution of ashes inserted between the latter two). Everybody expressed delight at the idea, and plans began accordingly.

A few days later, I received a call from one of the lay chaplains who explained that when she relayed our plan to the priest-director of the Office of Campus Ministry (her boss), he was displeased and insisted that a Mass be celebrated on Ash Wednesday evening. My recollection is that I was a bit surprised that she had to run the plans by him for his approval, but on the other hand I found myself not completely surprised that a priest was insistent that ashes be ministered during Mass. You see, just a few years before, during my last year of doctoral studies when I was earning my room and board in residence at a local parish, the pastor had in similar fashion inextricably tied conferring ashes to celebrating Mass, for which there would be the normal two early morning weekday Masses, a noon Mass (which he asked me to take, saying it would be standing room only, with loads of people from nearby office parks), plus an early evening Mass. I had the temerity (of youth, I'd like to suppose) of asking why all these Masses on a day not requiring them and, more to the point, whether the people coming from the workplaces at midday could afford the time for an entire

14. See Connerton, *How Societies Remember*, 22–29, 36, 84, 88.

Mass. He said that, unfortunately, some would show up late and leave early, but that did not detract from the necessity of Mass, which he asserted as obvious (and final!). For my part that noon, seeing the packed house before me, I explained in the opening rite that the Church requires that ashes be distributed in conjunction with the proclamation of God's word, but that remaining for the Liturgy of the Eucharist, while warmly encouraged, was nonetheless optional. People either pressed for time or not disposed to receiving Holy Communion, I advised, should not feel guilty about departing at the conclusion of the Liturgy of the Word. A palpable sigh of relief (variably expressed) quietly rose and subsided. Later, probably a third of the people left before the Liturgy of the Eucharist began. I believed I had met the pastor's directive while also meeting the pastoral needs of the people.

Such is my little tale, but it is loaded with theological implications, the extent of which well-exceed what I can address. Here I shall only attempt an initial overview of the sorts of power evident in the scenarios, which will then lead to a more extended consideration of the symbolism of Ash Wednesday itself. In thinking how to break down the whole into parts, I take as a heuristic guide the Constitution on the Sacred Liturgy's description of the multiple ways Christ is present in the enactment of the Church's rites.[15] Surely this divine-human presence implies power, the means through which, in the power of the Holy Spirit (the Constitution teaches), God is glorified and the people sanctified. The modes of presence include the sacramental minister, the symbols of the sacrament being celebrated (with that presence being unique in the case of eucharistic elements), the proclamation of word in Scripture, and the people themselves gathered in prayer and song.

The exercise of various types of power in ministerial leadership is evident not only on the obvious point that each scenario entailed a Mass and, thus, the priestly office and charism, per the Roman Catholic Church, lo these many centuries. But in each case the exercise of pastoral authority by the campus ministry director and the pastor were likewise in play. And part of the drama in the situations had to do with the difference in how I understood the pastoral-theological-liturgical situation in contrast to those two men. On the primary theological terrain of actual Catholic communities, we are very much still in what no doubt will be an extended period of varying interpretations of the general instructions of the official rites and the other doctrinal and procedural directives on divine worship

15. See Paul VI, *Sacrosanctum Concilium*, nos. 7, 33.

coming from the Vatican and local bishops—even as these rites and their introductions are in processes of revision all over again. These touch on every facet of theology (Christology, pneumatology, ecclesiology, anthropology, biblical revelation and interpretation). The Vatican has, in addition, given directives on the possibilities and limits of lay pastoral and liturgical ministries. Such instruction arises occasionally, occasioned by contestation over emergent local practices judged by the bishops to need regulation or prohibition. Myself, I find the 2004 Vatican instruction *Redemptionis Sacramentum* breathtaking in its scope and detail (enumerating multiple abuses to be abrogated).[16] Then, obviously, arises consideration here of the entire notion of priesthood in relation to the clerical caste and how it is circumscribed. Not only have many of the issues been polarizing, some have alienated people—laity, especially women, but also many of the ordained.

To note, then, briefly the laity: The liturgical assembly, formed by a multitude or few, perhaps especially in all diversities, is a powerful symbol indeed. In fact, the assembly is the basic symbol upon which all the rites depend. I shall say a bit more about the theological characteristics of assembling in prayer and song a bit later, but here I would just note the uncontested assumption by all in both scenarios that liturgical assembling is essential to the celebration (the ritual performance) of Ash Wednesday. Why is that? Why not just have people drop in for ashes at a drive-through window or street corner (per scattered practices of Episcopal and Protestant churches), as has been gleefully reported in the press in recent years?[17] One last note in relation to the assembly: Surely the kind of moral and even religious authority people accord the clergy covers a spectrum, with people quietly but openly doing their own thing in ways previously unimagined.

Of monumental importance and impact in the liturgical reform Vatican II set in motion was the augmentation of the Liturgy of the Word in the Mass, as well as the prescription that all the rites of the Church include the proclamation of Scripture. This, to my mind, has unleashed powers of revelation beyond human measure. What *can* be measurably observed is the amount of time and care now widely devoted to the celebration of the word, most extensively in the Mass (with the fulsome lectionary cycles, expanded numbers of readings, psalmody, *and* the liturgical homily). Ours

16. See Congregation for Divine Worship, *Redemptionis Sacramentum*, nos. 173–75.

17. It turns out there now exists a website, "Ashes To Go: taking worship to the streets," providing information for obtaining ashes at street locations (as well as train platforms, outside supermarkets and coffee shops) in some thirty-one US states and the District of Columbia: http://ashestogo.org/about/.

is a very different Mass now from that of 1962. And over the decades the impact has been widespread: People hear a full range of the gospels and, however poor the preaching may be, they hear *in the midst of the assembly* and the context of their personal life stories, for example, about Jesus feeding multitudes, befriending and dining with sinners (social outcasts), etc., leading them to pose serious questions about Roman liturgical law's restrictions on who may or may not receive Holy Communion and in what venues. But that is just one notably contested example. With regard to these Ash Wednesday scenarios, my own priority for the day's liturgy was about high-quality proclamation and response to the word, leading into the procession (the people's corporate movement together) and reception of the ashes (the word written on the body, per Chauvet). Whether I was (or am) right or wrong on this point, I do think the symbolic impact of doing this sacramental gesture alone (that is, without the further celebration of the sacrament of the Eucharist) would enhance the power of the ritual. This, again, is a complex idea, not least due to the question of whether the Mass (or Eucharist), while the apex of the Church's liturgical life, may not have evolved into a *de facto* requirement for the celebration of *any* rite to be experienced as divinely powerful.

Fearful that the above run-through of power issues has been so cursory and suggestive as to disappoint, I want nevertheless to use the time remaining to consider, then, the symbol of Ash Wednesday itself, doing this as an exercise in the pastoral-liturgical theology.

We would do well not to underestimate the power of the symbol of Ash Wednesday. If we think liturgy in this case first of all in terms of the liturgical calendar, the Church Year, then Ash Wednesday ranks among the top three in North American Catholicism, across the spectrum of ethnicities. While not dismissing festival days that are highly important (because so richly celebrated) within particular ethnic groups, such as Our Lady of Guadalupe, I am arguing here in terms of liturgical days universally observed on the popular level. Easter and Christmas are big, for sure, but just as with those holidays, Ash Wednesday is a day that Catholics who do not attend Sunday Mass regularly (let alone weekly) nonetheless take note of and participate in. The secular press and now wider social media are annually abuzz when the day arrives, and this is no small thing, this attentiveness to the event, given the fact that the particular date on the calendar changes annually. Media outlets "get" that this day is a powerfully defining one in the "social imaginary" of Roman Catholics and many other Christians.

To think of this in terms of a contemporary Catholic "social imaginary" is to employ Charles Taylor's concept for the pre-theoretical shared images, stories, and symbols whereby a group or society shape their common understanding and practices, lending them their legitimacy.[18] The media—exercising so much power in relation to fame, wealth, office (politics), word, and image—they "get" Ash Wednesday because believers "do" it in such visible numbers (and one must ponder how the secular media thereby empowers the Christian symbol). The practice is widely described as the beginning of the most holy season of the Christian Year, and the season as forty days of fasting and prayerful reflection (but not, at least to my attentive eyes and ears, of almsgiving). Yet few Catholics literally, actually fast—that is, cut their food consumption to one meal and two small snacks per day—for forty days or even on the two days that Church law mandates such bodily ritual observance by healthy adults—Ash Wednesday and Good Friday. Larger numbers may abstain from meat (with a nod to Mary Douglas and her affection for the Bog Irish)[19] on Ash Wednesday and Lenten Fridays, but to my observation even this has trailed off among the younger generations. I bring this up not to decry laxity but to keep a sharp eye on what motivates Catholic and other Christians in actual practice and, thereby, what one can reasonably deduce is powerful about their faith for their identity, for their personal, interpersonal, and social agency.

"Did you get your ashes?" I recall some years ago how a twenty-something friend, a youth social worker living and serving a severely troubled South Boston (think poverty, low educational attainment, high suicide rates), became so agitated over how everybody around her on Ash Wednesday, young and old, kept asking that question of each other. She hated what she, as nearly the only person of her or the next older generation present weekly at Sunday Mass, saw as hypocrisy. I think it is fair to say that she saw the fuss over getting to a church for a smudge of ashes on the forehead as an empty, inauthentic symbol. Ah, but therein lies the rub.

To think of the power of ritual and symbol, with Bell and the theorists she enlists, in terms of activity within a social body, creating and sustaining and gradually morphing the identity and agency of the members *by their very participation therein*, is to resist the modern temptation to prioritize thought over action, mind over body, supposedly autonomous individual over social institutions. The enthusiasm for Ash Wednesday participation,

18. See Taylor, *Secular Age*, 171–72.
19. See Douglas, *Natural Symbols*, 39–56.

past and present, for so many includes, often primarily entails, a profound sense of belonging, of Catholic self-and-mutual identification through performance. Canon Law and doctrinal instruction concerning Sunday Mass attendance or fasting and abstinence or confessing serious sin in sacramental penance before receiving Holy Communion—the accurate comprehension and careful following of these do not, it would seem, carry nearly as much weight in popular practice of Catholicism, in the ritual bodies of Catholics, as does the inscription of ashes on foreheads one wintry Wednesday per year.

As another team of social scientists have put it, modernity in all its sectors—academic, institutional, popular—has been mistaken in assuming the extent to which precision of thought governs people's lives. Adam Seligman and associates place *ritual* (broadly conceived) at one end of the human continuum for "framing experience, action, and understanding," while at the other end—and in ongoing tension—is what they call *sincerity*, which values individual decision and the exercise of the will, the workings of which "are singular, unique, discursive, and indicative to the highest degree."[20] Human ritual negotiates ambiguity without completely resolving it, as would, in contrast, a discursive (that is, sincere) explanation. Indeed, the ambiguity that haunts all boundaries in life—physical, social, traditional—is the very reason for ritualizing.[21] To quote Seligman and associates once more: "Ritual's repeated, performative, and antidiscursive nature . . . provides a critical way of dealing with, rather than overcoming, the eternal contradiction and ambiguity of human existence."[22]

Ritual is the way we humans hold the many irresolvable ambivalences of life in a *both-and* tension that orients and, with repetition, reorients people's identity and agency amidst the ambiguities of interpersonal, social, and cosmic relations, as well as through the changes in the individual life cycle—with death always looming around the edges. Attention to such human activity does not lend itself well to the pursuit of certitude through pure argument, nor to apodictic assertions about the singular proper execution of a given rite and its meaning.

20. Seligman et al., *Ritual*, 7, 118.
21. Seligman et al., *Ritual*, 41–47.
22. Seligman et al., *Ritual*, 129–30.

Conclusion: Liturgy Empowering Life in/for the World

In light of this line of theorizing, the symbolic power of Ash Wednesday for Roman Catholics and many other Christians becomes quite evident. The day with its primary symbol all but revels in the ambiguity of human life (for which the theological symbols are sin and death), inscribing it on the body—on the face, no less. The standard Catholic ritual prior to the post-Vatican II reform was for a priest simply to be standing in front of the sanctuary for posted hours at a time, with individuals coming down the aisle to have him perfunctorily press a thumb of ashes to one's forehead while solemnly proclaiming, "Remember man that thou art dust and unto dust thou shall return." I think it's fair to say that the conceptual and imaginal input the ritual offered the individual was quite minimal. *Memoria mortis*, indeed, and in light of that mortality take stock of one's life. In one sense, there is not much explicitly Christian in such a symbolic gesture, unless one takes into further account the bodily sensation of walking down the aisle of the church, the sacred Catholic space, with the pews all empty, to place oneself in the hand of the Christ-bearing priest. And those surely are no small factors.

Be that as it may, the historical fact is that the Second Vatican Council's mandated reform and renewal of the liturgy included making proclamation of the word of God integral to the celebration of every and all rites. Priority was likewise to be given to the corporate, communal nature of the Church in its assembled members, among whom full, conscious, and active participation is to be fostered. These, as well as a clergy educated in and imbued with the "spirit and power"[23] of the liturgy comprised the fundamental components of liturgical practice that could produce a reformed and renewed Catholic social imaginary, and this as needed amidst a rapidly changing, pluralistic world.

Hence the change in how the ritual conferring of ashes is to take place on Ash Wednesday. A genuine liturgy, that is, a work of service by and for the benefit of the people of God, is for Roman Catholicism now the only ordinary way for celebrating the first day of Lent, including the conferral of ashes. Why this need for assembling? This is the sign that people do not go it alone but, rather, as members of Christ's body, responsible to and for one another. The power in numbers, even just two or three gathered in Christ's name, cannot be gainsaid. One way to look at the need for such assembling

---

23. See Paul VI, *Sacrosanctum Concilium*, no. 14.

is the changing context, the pluralistic and rapidly secularizing world in which believers strive to live the faith. Assembling in symbolically significant sacred space, synchronizing individual person-bodies into a common, shared range of bodily vibration by means of music (heard but, for even greater effect, sung), falling together into habituated patterns of corporate silence and listening and vocal prayer,[24] by doing all of this, the people are not producing something external to themselves but rather, to follow Bell's persuasive theory, they are producing (or performing) themselves as the body of Christ, in his many members.

This must not, nonetheless, be sectarian, that is, a community closed in upon themselves. Paul, the apostolic author responsible for the symbolism of the church as Christ's body, himself had to convert the social imaginaries of the wealthier Christians in Corinth to recognize economic-class enclaves had no legitimacy in the local church body. Each local assembly, furthermore, needed to develop a sense of themselves, in their very ritual bodies sharing in the sacred mysteries, as symbolic of the universal church. Liturgical practice with those present, closest to them, through ritual word and deed was to broaden their vision toward and solidarity (communion) with those physically afar. Paul's taking up the collection for the struggling Jerusalem community, making his appeal not only in person but through his letters being read in the liturgically assembled community, is indicative of the symbolic power the ritualization of word, water bath, anointing, meal, and intercessory prayer could have for motivating love of one another and the wider others. Within the social and political conditions under which they lived, those earliest Christians were in their liturgy, to borrow a phrase from the liturgical theologian Aidan Kavanagh, "doing the world" as God intended it.[25] The post-Vatican II reformed emphasis on the active participation of all the liturgical assembly seeks to foster a similarly powerful social imaginary for contemporary believers. The readings for Ash Wednesday's liturgy of the word seek to reorient the community, with Paul exhorting the Corinthians to be reconciled to one another as Christ has reconciled humanity with God (2 Cor 5:20—6:2), and then Jesus instructing on practices of prayer, fasting, and almsgiving to be done without drawing attention (Matt 6:1–6, 16–18).

Neither did the early Christians nor do we today ever "do the world" in the liturgy perfectly. Theological reflection on this human fact of

24. See Morrill and Goodrich, "Liturgical Music," 20–36.

25. See Kavanagh, *On Liturgical Theology*, 52–71.

ritualizing, I would propose, resides in the scandal of the crucified and risen Christ, of the God revealed therein, whose ways are such as to place the baptized in an ongoing eschatologically tense life, rife with ambiguities and, yes, longings, founded on the promises borne of God's having taken into glory the humanity of the executed Nazarene. Irenaeus and other ancient pastors, when faced with the ambiguities of evil and suffering, wrote of God as longsuffering which, to my mind, invites deep personal and communal reflection. But there also at the church's origins is the apocalyptic cry, as Johann Baptist Metz paraphrases the close to the book of Revelation, "God, what are you waiting for? Come, and soon!"[26] The theology in the documents of Vatican II centers on the paradoxical divine-human power of the paschal mystery. I close by asserting that to be the hermeneutical key for theologically interpreting the liturgy's power in all the ambiguities of its performances and contexts.

26. See Metz, *Passion*, 58, 71, 84.

Bibliography

Athanasius. "Third Discourse Against the Arians." In *Athanasius: Select Works and Letters*, edited by Archibald Robertson, 393–432. Nicene and Post-Nicene Fathers, Second Series 4. Grand Rapids, MN: Eerdmans, 1987.

———. "Life of Antony." In *Athanasius: Select Works and Letters*, edited by Archibald Robertson, 188–221. Nicene and Post-Nicene Fathers, Second Series 4. Grand Rapids, MN: Eerdmans, 1987.

———. "On the Incarnation of the Word." In *Athanasius: Select Works and Letters, Bishop of Alexandria*, edited by Archibald Robertson, 31–67. Nicene and Post-Nicene Fathers, Second Series 4. Grand Rapids, MN: Eerdmans, 1987.

Baggett, Jerome P. *Sense of the Faithful: How American Catholics Live Their Faith*. New York: Oxford University Press, 2009.

Baldovin, John F. *Reforming the Reform: A Response to the Critics*. Collegeville, MN: Liturgical, 2009.

———. "Review of *Sacraments & Sacramentality*, by Bernard Cooke, and *Introduction to the Sacraments*, by John P. Schanz." *Worship* 58:6 (1984) 549–51.

Barras, Philippe. "Sacramental Theology at the Mercy of Pastoral Service." In *Sacraments: Revelation of the Humanity of God: Engaging the Fundamental Theology of Louis-Marie Chauvet*, edited by Philippe Bordeyne and Bruce T. Morrill, 83–100. Collegeville, MN: Liturgical, 2008.

Belcher, Kimberly Hope. *Efficacious Engagement: Sacramental Participation in the Trinitarian Mystery*. Collegeville, MN: Liturgical, 2011.

———. "Sacramentality and Foundational Experience: A Rreflection on Bruce Morrill's *The Essential Writings of Bernard Cooke*." *Pray Tell*, August 1, 2016. http://www.praytellblog.com/index.php/2016/08/01/sacramentality-and-foundational-experience-a-reflection-on-bruce-morrills-the-essential-writings-of-bernard-cooke/.

Bell, Catherine. *Ritual Theory, Ritual Practice*. New York: Oxford University Press, 1992.

Berger, Teresa. *Gender Differences and the Making of Liturgical History*. Burlington, VT: Ashgate, 2011.

———. *Women's Ways of Worship: Gender Analysis and Liturgical History*. Collegeville, MN: Liturgical, 1999.

Bieler, Andrea, and Luise Schottroff. *The Eucharist: Bodies, Bread, and Resurrection*. Minneapolis: Fortress, 2007.

Boeve, Lieven. "Theology in a Postmodern Context and the Hermeneutical Project of Louis-Marie Chauvet." In *Sacraments: Revelation of the Humanity of God: Engaging the Fundamental Theology of Louis-Marie Chauvet,* edited by Philippe Bordeyne and Bruce T. Morrill, 5–24. Collegeville, MN: Liturgical, 2008.

Bordeyne, Philippe. "The Ethical Horizon of Liturgy." In *Sacraments: Revelation of the Humanity of God: Engaging the Fundamental Theology of Louis-Marie Chauvet,* edited by Philippe Bordeyne and Bruce T. Morrill, 119–36. Collegeville, MN: Liturgical, 2008.

Bordeyne, Philippe, and Bruce T. Morrill. "Baptism and Identity Formation: Convergences in Ritual and Ethical Perspectives: A Dialogue." *Studia Liturgica* 42 (2012) 154–75.

Bornkamm, Gunther. *Early Christian Experience.* London: SCM, 1969.

Boselli, Goffredo. *The Spiritual Meaning of the Liturgy: School of Prayer, Source of Life.* Translated by Barry Hudock. Collegeville, MN: Liturgical, 2014.

Bradshaw, Paul F. *The Search for the Origins of Christian Worship: Sources and Methods for the Study of Early Liturgy.* 2nd ed. New York: Oxford University Press, 2002.

Brown, Peter. *The Body and Society: Men, Women, and Sexual Renunciation in Early Christianity.* New York: Columbia University Press, 1988.

Bullivant, Stephen. *Mass Exodus: Catholic Disaffiliation in Britain and America Since Vatican II.* Oxford: Oxford University Press, 2019.

Cabié, Robert. *Eucharist.* Vol. 2 of *The Church at Prayer.* Edited by A. G. Martimort. Translated by Matthew O'Connell. Collegeville, MN: Liturgical, 1986.

Carey, Patrick W. "Two Pioneers in Theological Education: Gerard S. Sloyan and Bernard J. Cooke." *U.S. Catholic Historian* 20:2 (2002) 223–47.

Center for Applied Research in the Apostolate (CARA). "Most Catholics Abstain from Eating Meat on Fridays during Lent." *CARA News,* March 11, 2008. http://cara. georgetown.edu/NewsandPress/PressReleases/pro31108.pdf.

———. "Sacrament of Reconciliation." *CARA News,* 2008. http://cara.georgetown.edu/ CARAServices/FRStats/reconciliation.pdf.

Chauvet, Louis-Marie. "Quand la théologie rencontre les sciences humaines." In *La responsabilité des théologiens. Mélanges offerts à Mgr J. Doré,* edited by F. Bousquet, 401–15. Paris: Desclée, 2002.

———. *The Sacraments: The Word of God at the Mercy of the Body.* Collegeville, MN: Liturgical, 2001.

———. *Symbol and Sacrament: A Sacramental Reinterpretation of Christian Existence.* Translated by Patrick Madigan and Madeleine Beaumont. Collegeville, MN: Liturgical, 1995.

Collins, Mary. "The Church and the Eucharist." *Catholic Theological Society of America Proceedings* 52 (1997) 19–34.

———. "Critical Questions for Liturgical Theology." *Worship* 53 (1979) 302–17.

Congregation for Divine Worship and the Discipline of the Sacraments. "Circular Letter Concerning the Integrity of the Sacrament of Penance." *Vatican.va,* March 12, 2000. http://www.adoremus.org/699Penance.html.

———. "Redemptionis Sacramentum: On Certain Matters to be Observed or to be Avoided Regarding the Most Holy Eucharist." *Vatican.va,* April 23, 2004. http:// www.vatican.va/roman_curia/congregations/ccdds/documents/rc_con_ccdds_ doc_20040423_redemptionis-sacramentum_en.html.

Connerton, Paul. *How Societies Remember.* Themes in the Social Sciences. Cambridge: Cambridge University Press, 1989.

Cooke, Bernard. "Body and Mystical Body: The Church as *Communio*." In *Bodies of Worship: Explorations in Theory and Practice*, edited by Bruce T. Morrill, 39–50. Collegeville, MN: Liturgical, 1999.

———. *The Distancing of God: The Ambiguity of Symbol in History and Theology*. Minneapolis: Fortress, 1990.

———. *Ministry to Word and Sacrament: History and Theology*. Philadelphia: Fortress, 1976/1980.

———. *Power and the Spirit of God: Toward an Experience-Based Pneumatology*. New York: Oxford University Press, 2004.

———. *Sacraments and Sacramentality*. Rev. ed. Mystic, CT: Twenty-Third, 1994.

Cooke, Bernard, and Bruce T. Morrill. *The Essential Writings of Bernard Cooke: A Narrative Theology of Church, Sacrament, and Ministry*. New York: Paulist, 2016.

Covino, Paul. "Christian Marriage: Sacramentality and Ritual Forms." In *Bodies of Worship: Explorations in Theory and Practice*, edited by Bruce T. Morrill, 107–19. Collegeville, MN: Liturgical, 1999.

Covino, Paul, and Austin Fleming. *Our Catholic Wedding*. Chicago: Liturgy Training, 2001. VHS.

Crainshaw, Jill Y. *Wise and Discerning Hearts: An Introduction to Wisdom Liturgical Theology*. Collegeville, MN: Liturgical, 2001.

Cyril of Alexandria. "The Third Letter of Cyril to Nestorius." In *Christology of the Later Fathers*, edited by Edward R. Hardy, 349. The Library of Christian Classics. Philadelphia: Westminster, 1954.

Dallen, James. *The Reconciling Community: The Rite of Penance*. Studies in the Reformed Rites of the Catholic Church 3. New York: Pueblo, 1986.

Dalmais, Irénée Henri, et al. *Principles of the Liturgy*. Vol. 1 of *The Church at Prayer*. Edited by Aimé Georges Martimort. Translated by Matthew O'Connell. Collegeville, MN: Liturgical, 1987.

Daly, Robert J. "Sacrifice Unveiled and Sacrifice Revisited: Trinitarian and Liturgical Perspectives." *Theological Studies* 64:1 (2003) 24–42.

D'Antonio, William V. et al. "American Catholics and Church Authority." In *The Crisis of Authority in Catholic Modernity*, edited by Michael J. Lacey and Francis Oakley, 273–92. New York: Oxford University Press, 2011.

Douglas, Mary. *Natural Symbols*. 2nd ed. New York: Routledge, 1996.

Dunn, James D. G. *Baptism in the Holy Spirit: A Reexamination of the New Testament Teaching on the Gift of the Spirit in Relation to Pentecostalism Today*. London: SCM, 1970.

———. *Romans 1–8*. Edited by David Allen Hubbard et al. Grand Rapids, MI: Zondervan Academic, 1988/2015.

Empereur, James L. *Prophetic Anointing: God's Call to the Sick, the Elderly, and the Dying*. Message of the Sacraments 3. Wilmington, DE: Michael Glazier, 1982.

Fagerberg, David W. *Theologia Prima: What Is Liturgical Theology?* 2nd ed. Chicago: Hillenbrand, 2004.

Farley, Margaret. "Beyond the Formal Principle: A Reply to Ramsey and Saliers." *Journal of Religious Ethics* 7:2 (1979) 191–202.

Farrow, Douglas. *Ascension and Ecclesia: On the Significance of the Doctrine of the Ascension for Ecclesiology and Christian Cosmology*. Grand Rapids, MI: Eerdmans, 1999.

Bibliography

Favazza, Joseph A. *The Order of Penitents: Historical Roots and Pastoral Future*. Collegeville, MN: Liturgical, 1988.

Foster, Charles R. *Educating Congregations: The Future of Christian Education*. Nashville: Abingdon, 1994.

Francis, Pope. *Laudato Si': On Care for Our Common Home*. Encyclical letter. *Vatican. va*, May 24, 2015. http://www.vatican.va/content/dam/francesco/pdf/encyclicals/documents/papa-francesco_20150524_enciclica-laudato-si_en.pdf.

Fuchs, Josef. *Human Values and Christian Morality*. Translated by M. H. Heelan et al. Dublin: Gill and Macmillan, 1970.

Geldhof, Joris. *Liturgy and Secularism: Beyond the Divide*. Collegeville, MN: Liturgical, 2018.

Gelpi, Donald. *Committed Worship: A Sacramental Theology for Converting Christians*. 2 vols. Collegeville, MN: Liturgical, 1993.

Gerhards, Albert, and Benedikt Kranemann. *Introduction to the Study of Liturgy*. Translated by Linda M. Maloney. Collegeville, MN: Liturgical, 2017.

Goizueta, Roberto S. *Caminemos con Jesús: Toward a Hispanic/Latino Theology of Accompaniment*. Maryknoll, NY: Orbis, 1995.

Gonsalves, Francis. *Feet Rooted, Hearts Radiant, Minds Raised: Living Sacraments in India*. Anand: Gujarat Sahitya Prakash, 2015.

Greeley, Andrew M. *The Catholic Imagination*. Berkeley: University of California Press, 2000.

Grimes, Ronald L. "The Scholarly Contexts and Practices of Ritual Criticism." In *Ritual Criticism: Case Studies in Its Practice, Essays on Its Theory*, 210–33. Columbia, SC: University of South Carolina Press, 1990.

Gutiérrez, Gustavo. *Essential Writings*. Edited by James B. Nickoloff. Maryknoll, NY: Orbis, 1996.

———. *The Power of the Poor in History*. Translated by Robert R. Barr. Maryknoll, NY: Orbis, 1983.

———. *A Theology of Liberation: History, Politics, and Salvation*. Rev. ed. Translated by Candad Inda and Matthew J. O'Connell. Maryknoll, NY: Orbis, 1988.

Handelman, Don. "Introduction: Why Ritual in Its Own Right? How So?" In *Ritual in Its Own Right: Exploring the Dynamics of Transformation*, edited by Don Handelman and Galina Lindquist, 1–32. New York: Berghahn, 2005.

Haquin, André. "The Liturgical Movement and Catholic Ritual Revision." In *The Oxford History of Christian Worship*, edited by Geoffrey Wainwright and Karen B. Westerfield Tucker, 696–720. New York: Oxford University Press, 2006.

Hellwig, Monika K. *Sign of Reconciliation and Conversion: The Sacrament of Penance for Our Times*. Message of the Sacraments 4. Wilmington, DE: Michael Glazier, 1982.

Himes, Michael J. "'Finding God in All Things': A Sacramental Worldview and Its Effects." In *As Leaven in the World: Catholic Perspectives on Faith, Vocations, and the Intellectual Life*, edited by Thomas M. Landy, 91–104. Franklin, WI: Sheed & Ward, 2001.

Hoffman, Lawrence. *Beyond the Text: A Holistic Approach to Liturgy*. Bloomington: Indiana University Press, 1987.

Holmgren, Frederick C. "Priests and Prophets: Spirituality and Social Conscience." *Worship* 79:4 (2005) 304–16.

Irwin, Kevin W. *Context and Text: Method in Liturgical Theology*. Collegeville, MN: Liturgical, 1994.

Bibliography

John Paul II, Pope. *Evangelium Vitae*. http://www.vatican.va/content/john-paul-ii/en/encyclicals/documents/hf_jp-ii_enc_25031995_evangelium-vitae.html.

———. *Misericordia Dei*. http://www.vatican.va/holy_father/john_paul_ii/motu_proprio/documents/hf_jp-ii_motu-proprio_20020502_misericordia-dei_en.html.

———. *Reconciliation and Penance*. http://www.vatican.va/holy_father/john_paul_ii/apost_exhortations/documents/hf_jp-ii_exh_02121984_reconciliatio-et-paenitentia_en.html.

Johnson, Elizabeth A. *She Who Is: The Mystery of God in Feminist Theological Discourse*. New York: Crossroad, 1992.

Johnson, Maxwell E. "Review of *Committed Worship*, by Donald Gelpi." *Worship* 68:5 (1994) 464–68.

Jordan, Mark D. *Teaching Bodies: Moral Formation in the Summa of Thomas Aquinas*. New York: Fordham University Press, 2017.

Kapferer, Bruce. "Ritual Dynamics and Virtual Practice: Beyond Representation and Meaning." In *Ritual in Its Own Right: Exploring the Dynamics of Transformation*, edited by Don Handelman and Galina Lindquist, 35–54. New York: Berghahn, 2005.

Kavanagh, Aidan. *On Liturgical Theology*. Collegeville, MN: Liturgical, 1990.

Kidder, Annemarie S. *Making Confession, Hearing Confession: A History of the Cure of Souls*. Collegeville, MN: Liturgical, 2010.

Lacey, Michael J. "Prologue: The Problem of Authority and Its Limits." In *The Crisis of Authority in Catholic Modernity*, edited by Michael J. Lacey and Francis Oakley, 1–25. New York: Oxford University Press, 2011.

Lathrop, Gordon W. *Holy People: A Liturgical Ecclesiology*. Minneapolis: Fortress, 1999.

———. *Holy Things: A Liturgical Theology*. Minneapolis: Fortress, 1993.

———. *Saving Images: The Presence of the Bible in Christian Liturgy*. Minneapolis: Fortress, 2017.

Léon-Dufour, Xavier. *Sharing the Eucharistic Bread: The Witness of the New Testament*. Translated by Matthew J. O'Connell. New York: Paulist, 1987.

McBrien, Richard P. *Catholicism*. Rev. ed. New York: HarperCollins, 1994.

Metz, Johann Baptist. *The Emergent Church: The Future of Christianity in a Post-Bourgeois World*. Translated by Peter Mann. New York: Crossroad, 1987.

———. *Faith in History and Society: Toward a Practical Fundamental Theology*. Rev. ed. Translated by J. Mathew Ashley. New York: Crossroad, 2007.

———. *A Passion for God: The Mystical-Political Dimension of Christianity*. Translated by J. Matthew Ashley. New York: Paulist, 1998.

———. *Poverty of Spirit*. Translated by John Drury and Carole Farris. Rev. ed. New York: Paulist, 1998.

Minear, Paul S. *To Heal and To Reveal*. New York: Seabury, 1976.

Mitchell, Nathan D. *Meeting Mystery: Liturgy, Worship, Sacraments*. Maryknoll, NY: Orbis, 2006.

———. *Mission and Ministry: History and Theology in the Sacrament of Order*. Message of the Sacraments 6. Wilmington, DE: Michael Glazier, 1982.

Moloney, Francis J. "Johannine Theology." In *The New Jerome Biblical Commentary*, edited by Raymond Brown et al., 1417–26. Englewood Cliffs, NJ: Prentice Hall, 1990.

Moltmann, Jürgen. *The Spirit of Life: A Universal Affirmation*. Translated by Margaret Kohl. Minneapolis: Fortress, 1992.

Morrill, Bruce T. *Anamnesis as Dangerous Memory: Political and Liturgical Theology in Dialogue*. Collegeville, MN: Liturgical, 2000.

Bibliography

————. "The Beginning of the End: Eschatology in the Liturgical Year and Lectionary." *Liturgical Ministry* 12 (Spring 2003) 65–74.

————. "Building on Chauvet's Work: An Overview." In *Sacraments: Revelation of the Humanity of God: Engaging the Fundamental Theology of Louis-Marie Chauvet*, edited by Philippe Bordeyne and Bruce T. Morrill, xv–xxiv. Collegeville, MN: Liturgical, 2008.

————. *Divine Worship and Human Healing: Liturgical Theology at the Margins of Life and Death*. Collegeville, MN: Liturgical, 2009.

————. *Encountering Christ in the Eucharist: The Paschal Mystery in People, Word, and Sacrament*. New York: Paulist, 2012.

————. "Les raisons pour lesquelles les Américains apprécient Louis-Marie Chauvet." *La Maison-Dieu* 267 (September 2011) 123–45.

————. "The Liturgical Is Political: A Narrative-Theological Assessment of Alexander Schmemann's Work." *Questions Liturgique/Study of Liturgy* 98 (2017) 41–59.

————. "Liturgical Music: Bodies Proclaiming and Responding to the Word of God." *Worship* 74:1 (2000) 20–36.

————. "Liturgical Theology as Critical Practice." *Spotlight on Theological Education* 2:1 (March 2008) 9–12.

————. "Liturgy, Ethics, and Politics: Constructive Inquiry into the Traditional Notion of Participation in Mystery." In *Mediating Mysteries, Understanding Liturgies: On Bridging the Gap Between Liturgy and Systematic Theology*, edited by Joris Geldhof, 187–206. Bibliotheca Ephemeridum Theologicarum Lovaniensium 278. Leuven: Peeters, 2015.

————. "The Many Bodies of Worship: Locating the Spirit's Work." In *Bodies of Worship: Explorations in Theory and Practice*, edited by Bruce T. Morrill, 19–37. Collegeville, MN: Liturgical, 1999.

————. "The Struggle for Tradition." In *Liturgy and the Moral Self: Humanity at Full Stretch Before God*, edited by E. Byron Anderson and Bruce T. Morrill, 67–77. Collegeville, MN: Liturgical, 1998.

Murphy-O'Connor, Jerome. "Eucharist and Community in First Corinthians." *Worship* 51 (1977) 56–69.

O'Meara, Thomas F., and Paul Philibert. *Scanning the Signs of the Times: French Dominicans in the Twentieth Century*. Adelaide: ATF, 2013.

The Order of Celebrating Matrimony. Collegeville, MN: Liturgical, 2016.

O'Toole, James. "Hear No Evil: Perhaps the Most Striking Development in the Practice of Confession in the U.S. Has Been Its Disappearance." *Boston College Magazine*, Fall 2000. http://bcm.bc.edu/issues/fall_2000/features.html.

Paul VI, Pope. *Dei Verbum*. https://www.vatican.va/archive/hist_councils/ii_vatican_council/documents/vat-ii_const_19651118_dei-verbum_en.html.

————. *Gaudium et Spes*. http://www.vatican.va/archive/hist_councils/ii_vatican_council/documents/vat-ii_const_19651207_gaudium-et-spes_en.html.

————. *Lumen Gentium*. http://www.vatican.va/archive/hist_councils/ii_vatican_council/documents/vat-ii_const_19641121_lumen-gentium_en.html.

————. *Sacrosanctum Concilium*. https://www.vatican.va/archive/hist_councils/ii_vatican_council/documents/vat-ii_const_19631204_sacrosanctum-concilium_en.html.

Power, David N. *The Eucharistic Mystery: Revitalizing the Tradition*. New York: Crossroad, 1992.

Bibliography

―――. *Sacrament: The Language of God's Giving*. New York: Crossroad, 1999.

―――. *The Sacrifice We Offer: The Tridentine Dogma and Its Reinterpretation*. New York: Crossroad, 1987.

―――. *Unsearchable Riches: The Symbolic Nature of Liturgy*. New York: Pueblo, 1984.

Power, David N., and Michael Downey. *Living the Justice of the Triune God*. Collegeville, MN: Liturgical, 2012.

Rahner, Karl. *The Church and the Sacraments*. Translated by W. J. O'Hara. New York: Herder & Herder, 1963.

―――. *Foundations of Christian Faith: An Introduction to the Idea of Christianity*. Translated by William V. Dych. New York: Crossroad, 1978.

Ramsey, Paul. "Liturgy and Ethics." *Journal of Religious Ethics* 7:2 (1979) 139–71.

Ratzinger, Joseph. "*Eschatologie und Utopie.*" *Internationale katholische Zeitschrift Communio* 6 (1977) 97–110.

Reid, Barbara E. "From Sacrifice to Self-Surrender to Love." *Liturgical Ministry* 18:2 (2009) 82–86.

Ricoeur, Paul. *Interpretation Theory: Discourse and the Surplus of Meaning*. Fort Worth: Texas Christian University Press, 1976.

―――. *The Symbolism of Evil*. Translated by Emerson Buchanan. Boston: Beacon, 1967.

"Rite of Marriage." In *The Rites of the Catholic Church*, 1:715–58. Collegeville: Liturgical, 1990.

"Rite of Penance." In *The Rites of the Catholic Church*, 1:517–629. Collegeville: Liturgical, 1990.

Ross, Susan A. *Extravagant Affections: A Feminist Sacramental Theology*. New York: Continuum, 2001.

Saliers, Don E. "Afterword: Liturgy and Ethics Revisited." In *Liturgy and the Moral Self: Humanity at Full Stretch Before God*, edited by E. Byron Anderson and Bruce T. Morrill, 209–24. Collegeville, MN: Liturgical, 1998.

―――. "Liturgy and Ethics: Some New Beginnings." *Journal of Religious Ethics* 7:2 (1979) 173–89.

―――. *Worship as Theology: Foretaste of Glory Divine*. Nashville: Abingdon, 1994.

Sammon, Margaret Ross. "The Politics of the U.S. Catholic Bishops: The Centrality of Abortion." In *Catholics and Politics: The Dynamic Tension Between Faith & Power*, edited by Kristin E. Heyer et al., 11–26. Washington, DC: Georgetown University Press, 2008.

Schillebeeckx, Edward. *Christ: The Christian Experience in the Modern World*. Vol. 7 of *The Collected Works of Edward Schillebeeckx*. Translated by John Bowden. Edited by Ted Schoof and Carl Sterkens. London: Bloomsbury T. & T. Clark, 2014.

―――. *Christ the Sacrament of the Encounter with God*. Translated by Mark Schoof and Laurence Bright. New York: Sheed & Ward, 1963.

―――. *Church: The Human Story of God*. Vol. 10 of *The Collected Works of Edward Schillebeeckx*. Translated by John Bowden. Edited by Ted Schoof and Carl Sterkens. London: Bloomsbury T. & T. Clark, 2014.

―――. *Interim Report on the Books Jesus and Christ*. Vol. 8 of *The Collected Works of Edward Schillebeeckx*. Edited by Ted Schoof and Carl Sterkens. London: Bloomsbury T. & T. Clark, 2014.

―――. *The Schillebeeckx Reader*. Edited by Robert J. Schreiter. New York: Crossroad, 1984.

Schmemann, Alexander. *The Eucharist: Sacrament of the Kingdom*. Translated by Paul Kachur. Crestwood, NY: St. Vladimir's Seminary Press, 1987.

———. *For the Life of the World: Sacraments and Orthodoxy*. Rev. ed. Crestwood, NY: St. Vladimir's Seminary Press, 1973.

———. *Introduction to Liturgical Theology*. Translated by Asheleigh Moorhouse. Crestwood, NY: St. Vladimir's Seminary Press, 1986.

———. *The Journals of Father Alexander Schmemann 1973–1983*. Edited by Juliana Schmemann. Crestwood, NY: St. Vladimir's Seminary Press, 2000.

Schmidt-Lauber, Hans-Christoph. "The Lutheran Tradition in the German Lands." In *The Oxford History of Christian Worship*, edited by Geoffrey Wainwright and Karen B. Westerfield Tucker, 395–421. New York: Oxford University Press, 2006.

Schnackenburg, Rudolph. *The Gospel according to St. John*. Vol. 1. Translated by Kevin Smyth. New York: Crossroad, 1982.

Schuth, Katarina. "Assessing the Education of Priests and Lay Ministers." In *The Crisis of Authority in Catholic Modernity*, edited by Michael J. Lacy and Francis Oakley, 318–47. New York: Oxford University Press, 2011.

Seligman, Adam B., et al. *Ritual and Its Consequences: An Essay on the Limits of Sincerity*. New York: Oxford University Press, 2008.

Smith, D. Moody. "John." In *Harper's Bible Commentary*, edited by James L. Mays, 1044–76. San Francisco: Harper & Row, 1988.

Sobrino, Jon. *No Salvation Outside the Poor: Prophetic-Utopian Essays*. Maryknoll, NY: Orbis, 2008.

———. *The Principle of Mercy: Taking the Crucified People from the Cross*. Maryknoll, NY: Orbis, 1994.

Souletie, Jean-Louis. "The Social Sciences and Christian Theology After Chauvet." In *Sacraments: Revelation of the Humanity of God: Engaging the Fundamental Theology of Louis-Marie Chauvet*, edited by Philippe Bordeyne and Bruce T. Morrill, 189–206. Collegeville, MN: Liturgical, 2008.

Spinks, Bryan D. "Anglicans and Dissenters." In *The Oxford History of Christian Worship*, edited by Geoffrey Wainwright and Karen B. Westerfield Tucker, 492–533. New York: Oxford University Press, 2006.

Spohn, William C. *Go and Do Likewise: Jesus and Ethics*. New York: Continuum, 2000.

Stotts, Jonathan. "Obedience as Belonging: Catholic Guilt and Frequent Confession in America." In *Sacramental Theology: Theory and Practice from Multiple Perspectives*, edited by Bruce T. Morrill, 85–104. Basel: MDPI, 2019.

Taft, Robert. "The Structural Analysis of Liturgical Units: An Essay in Methodology." *Worship* 52:4 (1978) 314–29.

Tannehill, Robert. *Dying and Rising in Christ*. Berlin: Alfred Topelmann, 1966.

Taussig, Hal. *In the Beginning Was the Meal: Social Experimentation and Early Christian Identity*. Minneapolis: Fortress, 2009.

Taylor, Charles. "Magisterial Authority." In *The Crisis of Authority in Catholic Modernity*, edited by Michael J. Lacey and Francis Oakley, 259–69. New York: Oxford University Press, 2011.

———. *A Secular Age*. Cambridge: Harvard University Press, 2007.

Taylor, Porter C., ed. *We Give Our Thanks unto Thee: Essays in Memory of Alexander Schmemann*. Eugene, OR: Pickwick, 2019.

Tentler, Leslie Woodcock. "Souls and Bodies: The Birth Control Controversy and the Collapse of Confession." In *The Crisis of Authority in Catholic Modernity*, edited by

Michael J. Lacey and Francis Oakley, 293–315. New York: Oxford University Press, 2011.

Theodore of Mopsuestia. "Baptismal Homily V." In *The Awe-Inspiring Rites of Initiation: The Origins of the RCIA*, by Edward Yarnold, 226–50. 2nd ed. Collegeville, MN: Liturgical, 1994.

Tillard, J.-M.-R. *Flesh of the Church, Flesh of Christ: At the Source of the Ecclesiology of Communion*. Translated by Madeleine Beaumont. Collegeville, MN: Liturgical, 2001.

Tracy, David. *The Analogical Imagination: Christian Theology and the Culture of Pluralism*. New York: Crossroad, 1989.

Tucker, Karen B. Westerfield. "North America." In *The Oxford History of Christian Worship*, edited by Geoffrey Wainwright and Karen B. Westerfield Tucker, 586–632. New York: Oxford University Press, 2006.

Wainwright, Geoffrey. "Ecumenical Convergences." In *The Oxford History of Christian Worship*, edited by Geoffrey Wainwright and Karen B. Westerfield Tucker, 720–54. New York: Oxford University Press, 2006.

———. *Eucharist and Eschatology*. New York: Oxford University Press, 1981.

Wannenwetsch, Bernd. *Political Worship: Ethics for Christian Citizens*. Translated by Margaret Kohl. Oxford: Oxford University Press, 2004.

Westermeyer, Paul. "Liturgical Music: *Soli Deo Gloria*." In *Liturgy and the Moral Self: Humanity at Full Stretch Before God*, edited by E. Byron Anderson and Bruce T. Morrill, 193–208. Collegeville, MN: Liturgical, 1998.

White, James F. "Forum: Lessons in Liturgical Pedagogy." *Worship* 68:5 (1994) 438–50.

———. *Roman Catholic Worship: Trent to Today*. Rev. ed. Collegeville, MN: Liturgical, 2003.

Wright, N. T. *Jesus and the Victory of God*. Christian Origins and the Question of God 2. Minneapolis: Fortress, 1996.

———. *The Resurrection of the Son of God*. Christian Origins and the Question of God 3. Minneapolis: Fortress, 2003.

Index

Index

Saliers, Don, 37, 91, 93–94, 127–31
sacrament, sacramental, 6, 11, 27, 67, 76, 82, 84, 126, 141
  definition of, 25, 73, 117, 137–38
  efficacy, power of, 12, 58, 69, 74–75, 110, 111, 113, 125, 140–42, 147
  See also theology
salvation, 9, 44, 104–06, 115, 117, 126, 137–38, 141
sanctification, ix, 25, 46, 105, 113–17, 119, 121, 126, 127, 141–42, 147
Schillebeeckx, Edward, 6, 102, 115–21, 141, 149
Schmemann, Alexander, 38, 100–101, 129
Schuth, Katarina, 70–71
Scripture. *See* word
Seligman, Adam, 13–15, 95, 97, 99, 158
sin, 30, 59–61, 64–70, 72, 76–79, 98, 136, 158
Sobrino, Jon, 135
society, 13, 15, 35, 65–66
  social class, 24, 31–32, 40, 109, 160
Sölle, Dorothee, 102
Souletie, Jean-Louis, 11–12
Spirit of God, 11, 59, 95, 97, 116–17, 126, 140, 151
  divine power, 38–39, 66, 74, 104–05, 108, 110, 112–13, 122, 135, 140, 150–51
  Holy Spirit, 38, 40, 61, 76–77, 85, 105, 108, 112, 114, 147
Spohn, William, 92, 128
suffering, 11, 104, 115–16, 118, 133–35, 161
  theodicy, 107, 136–37
symbol, symbolism, 11, 51, 100, 105, 130, 133, 135
  power in/of, 25, 46, 50, 69, 126, 138–39, 157, 159

Taft, Robert, 9n20, 44
Taylor, Charles, 132, 157
  social imaginary, 125, 156–57, 159–60
Theodore of Mopsuestia, 113–14

theology
  biblical, 95–100, 124–26, 131, 136–37
  liberation, 4–5, 65, 102, 117, 119, 134–35
  liturgical-sacramental, 3–18, 21–22, 37–38, 55–56, 68–69, 93, 100–101, 104, 127–29, 137, 146, 149–52
  magisterial, official Catholic, 29, 34, 59, 64–68, 76
  patristic, 78, 105, 109–10, 112–13, 115, 136, 161
  political, 4–5, 102, 115, 119, 132–33, 135–37
Tillard, J.-M.-R., 126
time, 81, 100–101, 108, 126–27. *See also* liturgy
Tracy, David, 4, 103n5
tradition, 11, 17, 23, 30, 33, 35, 39, 43, 50, 78, 85, 101, 124, 130, 151
truth, 12, 13, 17, 49, 73, 100–01

Vatican Council II
  Constitutions
    Church, 40, 67n48
    Church in Modern World, 26n9, 40, 108
    Divine Revelation, 39
    Sacred Liturgy, 7, 9, 48, 51, 54, 104, 124–25, 127, 141, 154, 159

Wannenwetsch, Bernd, 42–43, 51
White, James, 6–7, 48
word
  biblical, 11, 17, 78, 90–91, 103, 105–9, 134–35, 139, 141–42, 151, 161
  divine, incarnate, 110–113, 151
  homiletics, preaching, 51, 85, 130, 141, 152–53, 156
  liturgy of, 42, 51, 103, 139–40, 154–56, 160
  proclamation of, 11, 39, 46, 138, 140, 159
worship, 11, 42, 101, 103, 105, 126–29